If your personal journey has had periods of personal brokenness, pain, and deep darkness, Layne Wallace's book will give you common ground and a healing guide through lament to faith. The great current relevance of this book is not only in its candor and insight, but that it is a pastor's journey. I am convinced that accounts of personal pain are inherently cathartic, and this one must have been. But the excellent writing and theological richness of these reflections will expand the capacities of empathy and the faith of any reader. With pain among dear ones all around us there is significant help and encouragement here.

—*Ronald L. Cook*
Associate Professor of Christian Scriptures
Director of Doctor of Ministry Program
Director of the W. Winfred Moore Center
for Ministry Effectiveness
Truett Seminary, Baylor University (retired)

Layne Wallace writes in this volume reflections of raw honesty as he and his family faced the darkness during the suffering and death of a beloved family member. He shares the emotions and feelings that hurting souls encounter when faced with such loss. Though his grief profound, Wallace came to see the care of God in new and meaningful ways. This book will be helpful counsel to all who journey in the darkness of grief and seek God's comfort.

—*Michael G. Cogdill*
Dean and Professor Emeritus
Campbell Divinity School
Buies Creek, North Carolina

Authentic and profound, hopeful and empowering. Layne invites us, with unflinching honesty, to a story he lived during an intense season of his life. At times depleted and barren but yet full of grit to labor over questions about God and ask questions to God that ultimately carried him to restoration, Layne's story empowers us, should we embrace the lessons found within, to hold to Christ no matter what foes arise in our journey. I'm looking forward to my second read-through!

—*Joshua Rose*
Group Life Pastor
Rush Creek Church

LOVING GOD IN THE DARKNESS

Smyth & Helwys Publishing, Inc.
6316 Peake Road
Macon, Georgia 31210-3960
1-800-747-3016
©2023 by Layne Wallace
All rights reserved.

Library of Congress Cataloging-in-Publication Data

Names: Wallace, Layne, 1973- author.
Title: Loving God in the darkness / by Layne Wallace.
Description: Macon, GA : Smyth & Helwys Publishing, [2023] | Includes
bibliographical references.
Identifiers: LCCN 2023000847 | ISBN 9781641734387 (paperback)
Subjects: LCSH: Resilience (Personality trait)--Religious
aspects--Christianity. | Suffering--Religious aspects--Christianity. |
Loss--Religious aspects--Christianity.
Classification: LCC BV4597.58.R47 W355 2023 | DDC
248.8/6--dc23/eng/20230512
LC record available at https://lccn.loc.gov/2023000847

LOVING
GOD
IN THE
DARKNESS

LAYNE WALLACE

Also by *Layne Wallace*

Karl Barth's Concept of Nothingness:
A Critical Evaluation

Dedicated to
Jennifer Rae Wallace Cornwell
November 20, 1982–March 23, 2009
Our "Ray of Sunshine"

Acknowledgments

To Molly and my girls: you fill my heart with joy daily. Life with you is the best kind of adventure.

To Rosemary Baptist Church: It is an honor to be your pastor. You have endured with me, prayed with me, and supported me since I became your pastor in 2009. I only hope I have been as good to you as you have been to me.

To Josh Cornwell: You are one of the bright lights in the world. I pray your every dream is fulfilled. I pray your every hope granted. Thanks for being the face of courage.

To Judi Wallace Russell: I'm so proud of you for all you have accomplished and the life you have created. You are an inspiration.

To Dad: I'm always impressed with your courage and strength. Thanks for every single thing you have taught me.

Contents

Preface

I want to tell you a story. It is a story about loss, about suffering, about pain, about God. In these pages you will meet people very dear to me: family, friends, a teacher. You will see some unvarnished and unpleasant views of my soul. You will see how someone can break, and you will see how someone can love God while living in darkness.

Since the beginning of the Christian faith, believers have divided the world between light and darkness. For millennia, believers have used the analogy that good is to evil as light is to darkness. Just as darkness is the absence of light, evil is the absence of good. It is a good analogy. When I refer to darkness in these pages, it is shorthand for the absence of good, the absence of God's presence, and the bitterness this absence causes.

The analogy is a good one, but it is not a perfect one. We experience light and darkness at regular intervals, so we might conclude that darkness is necessary. Night must follow day. Therefore, without the darkness we would be incomplete. There are things we have learned in the darkness. Darkness, therefore, must be necessary for us. But the Bible does not use this logic. This logic presses the analogy too far. God is not so much keeping the darkness in balance as God is working to destroy the works of darkness. If we learn and grow from the darkness, it is because God is at work causing even evil to function for our good. God does not send evil and darkness. No, God outwits and overwhelms the darkness. If the victory is not visible now, it will be in the eternity to come.

In these pages you will see how I learned to love God even when the darkness of God's absence blinded me to all that is good and right. My wish for you is that you never know this darkness. If you do, however, I want you to know that even in the darkness, God is with you.

CHAPTER 1

The Light Goes Out

The sign said "9200 Family Waiting," but it might as well have read, "Abandon all hope ye who enter here." It was the kind of place that could lead one to conclude that hell and hospitals have the same interior decorator. There were only a few empty chairs in 9200 Family Waiting, as many families stayed in the room to care for their loved ones. There were yellowish-brown stains from spilt drinks on the tile floor that had not been mopped in several days. There were empty coffee cups on the end table in the corner. The florescent lights were somehow dim, which made the room feel uncomfortable. The tan, faux leather chairs lined the perimeter of the room, making any sort of comforting conversation difficult. The room was warm and stuffy; it felt like a human petri dish. Some families had rearranged a few of the chairs so they could stretch out their legs to try to get comfortable and attempt to get some sleep.

In 9200 Family Waiting, the only comfort was in information, and information was in short supply. The doctors did their rounds without the families in their loved ones' rooms. So the families had to rely on listening to nurses' summaries or finding the doctors later in the day for conferences. At times, waiting in the dirty, stuffy, crowded room was intolerable. The only escape was to step outside of the room for air.

That is where I saw Josh, my sister Jenni's husband. He was leaning on the door frame and talking to his mother. His over six-foot frame towered over her as they spoke. He was wearing khaki cargo pants and his standard University of North Carolina T-shirt, a brave choice at Duke University Medical Center. Although he was young, in his mid-twenties, he looked haggard. He hadn't shaved in days, and the weight of what was occurring visibly weighed him down. He could barely lift his head. It was March 13, 2009, and the struggle for Jenni's survival since March 1 had clearly wearied him.

I had known Josh for several years, and I had learned to have deep respect for him. He had come home from college with my sister Jenni, and apparently they were a "thing." Jenni and Josh met for the first time during mock interviews for the North Carolina Teaching Fellows Program. The program was designed to recruit great students to become teachers in the North Carolina public school system. It paid a full scholarship to several North Carolina public universities. Jenni was already a teaching fellow and was giving high school seniors a tour of her campus. Josh was on one of Jenni's tours, and that is where they met. When Josh entered the program the following fall, he thought he had no chance with Jenni, as she was clearly interested in some upper-classmen who were vying for her attention. One of the guys interested in Jenni was involved in the card game Magic. Jenni was not proficient at the game, but she taunted him, saying how she would beat him the next time they played. Josh overheard the conversation and said, "If you really want to beat him, I can show you how." They bonded.

An evening a few weeks later, Jenni, visibly upset, was walking around campus. Josh saw her and spoke with her. Somehow the subject of dating came up. Josh said, "I don't want to miss an opportunity for a great relationship just to save a friendship." Crickets. In Josh's words it was "super awkward." Jenni said nothing. Josh, thinking he was stuck in the "friend zone" forever, said, "Okay. You've got to give me something." With that, they started dating. It was near Easter.

By Thanksgiving they were dating seriously, and Josh came to our family festivities. Being introduced as a boyfriend to the family is always unnerving, and with my raucous clan it was probably more than a bit intimidating. Josh, though, handled the situation with class. We all liked him immediately. The following Christmas, Jenni brought home something else along with Josh—sickness. She came home with a terrible raspy voice. We all thought it was mono, something that runs rampant on college campuses. We insisted that she go to the doctor. She agreed and said she had already been trying to get medical help. At first, she got very little. The campus physician accused Jenni of feigning sickness in order to get out of going to class. Everyone who knew Jenni's intelligence and studious nature found the doctor's accusation laughable. No, something was wrong, and answers were not forthcoming.

Jenni's condition continued to deteriorate, and she became terribly ill. She finally vomited blood and went to the emergency room. When the doctor looked at the results of Jenni's chest x-ray, his demeanor changed abruptly. He immediately wanted to talk to my father. After getting him in the room, he announced the diagnosis. Jenni did not have mono; she had non-Hodgkin's lymphoma.

There is no news worse than hearing that your loved one has cancer. It terrified the entire family. As quickly as I could break away from my responsibilities as pastor, I made a trip home to spend time with Jenni. Jenni did not seem worried. I wished I could say the same.

I'm sure Josh was worried too. One could expect that her diagnosis might have been too heavy for a college kid like Josh. After all, he should have been enjoying his college years. He should have been carefree and without major responsibility. He would be expected to flinch at this diagnosis. In fact, some of Josh's acquaintances insinuated that he should cut Jenni loose. They would ask how he could be that invested in someone he had dated for only a few months. The implication was that Josh had little invested in Jenni and Jenni was sick, so why not find a healthy girlfriend? Josh never gave the response he thought the question deserved: "You are so callous. What gives you the right to ask that question?" One could have expected him to run from the drama and weight of a cancer diagnosis. If one had expected such things, one would have been wrong. Josh stood by Jenni. Her course of treatment was chemotherapy and radiation, and with him by her side she handled it beautifully. She even earned a 4.0 while undergoing chemotherapy.

Jenni recovered from this bout with lymphoma and excelled in her studies, graduating from college. During her time in college, Jenni and Josh became more than an item; they clearly loved each other. When Jenni announced that she and Josh were engaged, the family was elated. Jenni and Josh had found each other, and the future looked very bright.

This bout with non-Hodgkin's lymphoma did make a deep impression on Josh, though. He thought, "Wow. What if this is a lot shorter than I want it to be? How can we make whatever we have meaningful because we may not have long?"

Jenni and Josh planned to get married in our hometown in our home church, Beverly Hills Baptist Church, in 2005.

But Jenni had begun to have symptoms again, and by the time their December wedding day arrived, we knew that the lymphoma had returned. I pronounced them husband and wife and fought back tears during the wedding homily.

As soon as Jenni and Josh returned from their honeymoon, the treatments began. Just as with the previous cancer, Jenni faced harsh treatments and physical difficulties. Just as before, Josh was with her. He bore the ravages of her cancer, chemotherapy, radiation, and nausea with great grace. We loved him for it. The treatments were successful. Jenni had now survived cancer twice, and she seemed to be doing quite well. The family breathed a sigh of relief, at least temporarily.

In October 2007, Jenni and Josh came to my daughter's second birthday party. After watching my daughter open gifts and eat cake, I was able to sit down and spend a few minutes alone with Jenni. While we were talking, I noticed something odd. One of her toes was in a spasm, and it was curled up unnaturally. I was alarmed, and I suggested that she go to the doctor immediately. While Jenni did not seem alarmed, she went to the doctor. The news could not have been worse. The radiation and chemotherapy that had saved Jenni's life caused a major complication. In about 5 percent of people who have non-Hodgkin's lymphoma, radiation and chemotherapy cause leukemia. Jenni was among the 5 percent.

The treatments for leukemia were different from Jennie's treatment for non-Hodgkin's lymphoma. This time, Jenni required a stem cell transplant. Amy, our older sister; Judi, Jenni's fraternal twin; and I were tested for compatibility. Surprisingly, among her siblings I was the closest match. I gladly agreed to donate the stem cells. The process of donation took several weeks. The doctors gave me regular injections to increase my production of T-cells, a kind of white blood cell in the bone marrow. Once I had enough of them, I was given an injection to force them into the bloodstream. It was uncomfortable. Every large bone ached, like I had the flu. One day later, I was ready to donate cells. While I was growing new T-cells, Jenni was receiving radiation and chemotherapy to eliminate her immune system so her body could receive mine. The transplant worked. Since Jenni had to grow a completely new immune system, she had to remain at Duke until her new system started working. It took several weeks, but finally Jenni was able to go home. The transplant was successful, and Jenni was now a three-time cancer survivor.

During the weeks and months that followed, Jenni's progress went well. She was able to live a fairly normal life, although with a stem-cell transplant no life is really normal. From time to time some complications would emerge, but they were treated, and it seemed that Jenni was doing well.

On March 1, 2009, Jenni entered Duke University Medical Center because some complications had become quite serious. She had developed graft-host symptoms in her eyes and mouth. She had developed diffuse alveolar hemorrhaging in her lungs. Thrombotic thrombocytopenic purpura was ravaging her blood, and the doctors seemed to believe that it was the source of her other issues.

On that same dark, bitterly cold rainy day, I was installed as the senior pastor at Rosemary Baptist Church in Roanoke Rapids, North Carolina. I was extremely proud that Jack Causey, the North Carolina pastor who had become a hero and mentor of mine, delivered the installation sermon. Professionally speaking, I was elated. I was going to serve the kind of church I had wanted to serve for some time. It should have been a momentous day, but with Jenni going into the hospital and with nagging worries in my home life, my celebration was muted. The conversation on the way back to my then home, an hour and a half from Roanoke Rapids, was as cold as the weather. Perhaps that distracted me from the seriousness of Jenni's condition. For whatever reason, it did not dawn on me just how grim her situation was. I believe psychologists call this reaction "denial."

In retrospect, it was obvious that things were not going well. Somehow, though, I always had the feeling that everything would be okay. Jenni had survived much worse, so I was certain she would come through this time too. I suppose it is normal to believe a three-time cancer survivor is invincible. As much as I did not want to admit it, this time was different.

When I arrived at 9200 Family Waiting, Josh struggled to say that the doctors were putting Jenni on a ventilator. They were unsure if she would ever be able to come off of it, but she could no longer survive without it.

Josh had begun a blog to help communicate Jenni's condition to her family and many friends. After reading a wrenching series of blog posts by Josh, I headed to Durham, North Carolina. Jenni and Josh needed me there—and had for some time. I wished I had arrived earlier.

By the time I came to the hospital to stay, Jenni had been there for twelve awful days. As the days wore on, any denial turned to heartbreak.

My congregation was gracious to me. I had barely unpacked my books when I had to drop everything for a personal crisis. They were the kind of prayerful and loving congregation that gives the faith a good name.

When I arrived, I realized just how difficult things had been at the hospital, particularly for Josh. Josh had many frustrations with the hospital staff. There were two main problems. The first was that he could not get good information about Jenni's condition. The hall where Jenni was receiving care was designed before the passing of HIPAA regulations.[1] Each room was divided by a wall, but in order to give medical professionals easier access to patients, there was no front wall. Because of this design, only a curtain protected the privacy of patients. A person could conceivably eavesdrop on a conversation the doctor was having with another patient. With HIPAA now law, Duke had created a policy that forced every family member out of the curtained rooms when the doctors were making rounds in order to protect confidentiality of other patients. That meant that the family could not listen to the doctors' discussions about the patients and could not ask questions in a timely manner.

The second issue was the attitude of the doctors and some of the nurses. Make no mistake, Duke Medical Center is one of the best hospitals in the world. The communication they gave to the family members at that time, however, was unacceptable. Once, Josh reported trying to see Jenni and speak to the doctor. The doctor was putting on his gown and gloves when he pointed at Josh and, without speaking to him, kicked him out. Josh also had encountered several nurses who were not sociable or kind. This occurred so frequently that Josh was relieved when Jenni's nurses had good attitudes.

With that backdrop, I listened to Josh struggle to tell us what was going to happen with Jenni. Still very confident that Jenni was going to be okay, I focused my attention on helping Josh and my family get through this crisis. I was worried about my dad. He had already buried a wife, our mother, twelve years earlier from cancer. Now, Jenni's repeated bouts with cancer were clearly wearing on him. I was worried about Jenni's twin, Judi. They had been close their entire lives, as one would expect with twins. Judi was in nursing school, and I wondered how she could focus when Jenni was so sick. I was also worried about Josh. As I looked at him, I thought that no person this young should have to go through such a nightmare. He was a kid. He was barely out of college. Jenni and Josh had been married only a few years. Where would he find the mental and emotional reserve to cope? Now that I was there, I was committed to do anything to help my sister, Josh, and my family.

I decided Jenni needed another advocate. I believed Josh was fully up to the task, but his attention needed to be elsewhere. He needed to focus on making medical decisions and on being emotionally present for Jenni. If there was a need to advocate on Jenni's behalf, I would do it. If there needed to be an uncomfortable conversation about Jenni's treatment, I planned to have it so Josh would not be distracted.

We were at Duke for days, and much of the time it felt like we were fighting the health care process. Most of the doctors lacked simple courtesy. Getting information was difficult, and getting simple questions answered was nearly impossible. On one of my visits with Jenni, a doctor was in the room, and I turned to him to ask a question about the drug heparin. The hemorrhaging in Jenni's lungs was the chief obstacle to her survival, and heparin prevents clotting. I wanted to ask him if the parts of Jenni's dialysis machine were treated with heparin as well. As I began to ask my question, he snarled, "Ask the nurse," without so much as blinking. I was livid. At the time I said that most of the doctors had the bedside manner of a disturbed cottonmouth.[2]

Finally, the emotions of the situation, the lack of information, the shoddy conditions of the waiting room, and the surly, arrogant nature of the medical professionals got to me. Eight days of maltreatment had gotten to me. I'd had *enough*. The flashpoint was the doctors' conversations about Jenni in Jenni's room. The doctors, believing that the situation was hopeless, were discussing disconnecting Jenni from life support *in Jenni's presence*. Jenni, although heavily medicated and on life support, was aware of the conversations in the room. In fact, during one visit I asked her if she wanted to listen to her mp3 player. She nodded. The idea that the doctors were discussing the removal of life support with Jenni able to hear made my blood boil. The family felt the same way.

Since I had promised that Josh would not have to confront the medical team about problems like that, I brought it up with the nurse who was working with Jenni that day.

"Is there any way you can ask the doctors not to talk about disconnecting Jenni in here?" I asked.

"I'm just the nurse," he growled.

"I know, but we're having a difficult time with this issue."

"You know, I really shouldn't be talking with you about her condition. Immediate family only."

"You were just talking with her mother-in-law. I'm her brother."

"I can't talk to you. It is a matter of ethics."

"Ethics?" I bellowed. "After the treatment Jenni and the family have been getting, don't talk to me about ethics." I fumed as I walked out of the room and headed down the hall to the waiting area, ranting loudly at the nurse.

Following me, he asked, "Do you have any training?"

With my rage piling up I yelled, "I have a doctorate," hoping he would not ask in what field I had my doctorate.

"Well, you're not immediate family, and I'm not talking to you anymore. You have made taking care of your very sick sister harder. Get out."

"I'm leaving!"

With fury taking over, I yelled some more incomprehensible gibberish in his direction and walked out. Frankly, I was somewhere between proud and embarrassed at my behavior. I should not have lost my temper, but I was proud that I fought for Jenni. I did not ask how other members of the family felt. I did note that some of the other families told me they wanted to applaud, as they had received similar treatment.[3]

A few moments later, several members of Duke security stepped in the hallway, and Josh was called out. As he walked out, I said, "They may throw me out of the hospital, but I want that nurse off the case." When the security team confronted him with my actions, he said that I was reflecting the concerns of the whole family. I was not thrown out, but I could not visit with Jenni alone anymore.

As I reflect on that event, I note one thing: *I was walking away.* I was not sporting for a fight. I was not trying to escalate the event. I was trying to leave. The nurse followed me to continue the argument. None of this is to say that losing my temper was right. I wish I had not. On the other hand, Jenni's life and dignity were in the balance. I would fight for those any time.

It was a gift of grace that some members Rosemary Baptist Church showed up later that day. In the aftermath of the event, Bernie and Myra Robertson took me to lunch in the hospital cafeteria. I was still seething, almost ranting. I had been their pastor for less than three weeks, and they did not think less of me because of what happened or recoil from my raw emotions. For that gift of grace, I remain grateful to this day.

After lunch, I was able to regroup. I went back to the waiting room. The family and I had discovered a treatment for patients with symptoms similar to Jenni's that had been designed by Danish doctors. The name of the treatment was Factor VII. We urged the doctors at Duke to look at the results. While the doctors were dubious, they carefully weighed the options. As they deliberated, we continued to look for other treatment possibilities. We continued to pray. We continued to work for Jenni's sake. We fought the good fight all the way to the end.

The next day Jenni's condition deteriorated even more. She had become so fragile that merely moving her caused life-threatening drops in her heart rate and blood pressure. When one hears the word "stable" in a medical situation, it is ordinarily a good thing. For Jenni it was not. "Stable" meant no significant change, and Jenni was running out of time. By nightfall, Josh wondered if it was the right thing to continue to fight for Jenni's survival. He wondered if it was "time," if we were hurting Jenni by continuing, if Jenni's wishes were being honored.

On Monday, March 23, 2009, it became apparent that Jenni would not recover. The doctors had run out of treatment options. The only thing we could do was discontinue the extraordinary measures we were employing to save her life. That afternoon, on the blog Josh had started to communicate Jenni's condition to her loved ones, I wrote,

> We just had a very sad conversation with Jenni's docs. Jenni's condition continues to deteriorate. They are out of treatment options. Factor VII given through the lungs was ruled out because the doctors believe it would cause a painful passing and would not help at all.
>
> Therefore, tonight when all the family can be gathered, we will discontinue the extraordinary means that we have used to keep Jenni going.

Jenni did not want to be on the vent for long, and she would not want to be on the machine if there were no hope of recovery. We are honoring her wishes.

Thank you for your love and prayers. The outpouring of support has been more than I can really comprehend. It has carried us through these difficult days. May God bless you.

The family gathered around the bedside. I sat in a chair by Jenni's side. While resting my forehead on the side of the bed, I held her hand. The machines were turned off; the beeping and bleeping that had filled our ears for days were silenced. We waited. Jenni's breathing steadily slowed and then stopped.

Just after 9:00 p.m., Jenni died. My beloved little sister was gone.

Jenni was quite the amazing person. She was beautiful, brilliant, spiritually deep, and good hearted. Jenni and her twin, Judi, came into this world on November 20, 1982, and they were a wonderful surprise. My mother had expected one boy. Lest you think this was before the age of modern medical technology, two separate sonograms indicated that there would be one son. Needless to say, when my mother went into labor prematurely, the situation was a bit dicey. The doctor ordered a new sonogram. He was completely flummoxed by what he saw. There were two babies. To this day, how the doctor reacted remains a family joke. My dad still imitates the doctor's Iranian accent: "Two babies, cannot understand it. Two babies, cannot understand it." When the two babies arrived, they did not even have names. They were simply called "A baby Wallace" and "B baby Wallace." Mom had picked out a name for one boy, not two girls!

I, however, was not impressed. I was ten years old and wanted a brother. If I was going to relinquish my status of being the baby in the family—the apple of my grandad's eye—I needed a brother. As I recall, I tried to trade Judi and Jenni to my uncle for an antique revolver. I was foiled. I'm pretty sure my mom was mortified that I would try such a thing. She never said anything, though. That Thanksgiving, just a few days after they were born, I got to see my little sisters for the first time. They were teeny, tiny little people who immediately took up a big space in our home and our hearts. We frequently just called them "the girls" or "the twins."

When Judi and Jenni came home, they were a handful—and not in a good way. They were sick, and for the first two years of their lives they pretty much screamed nonstop. My grandmother used to say that for those first two years, "They were hard to even like." But they got past that. They grew to be whole and healthy and a giant mess.

I recall one summer Sunday afternoon when the family was in the den watching TV. It occurred to us that we had not heard from the girls in a while. As a matter of fact, the house was eerily quiet. Realizing the quiet was a problem, my dad quickly rushed to the girls' room. He discovered that Judi and Jenni had gotten into some fingernail polish. They had painted themselves, their dresser, and the brand-new carpet in their room. The string of profanities that came out of my father's mouth would have made the whole Navy blush. To this day, I'm not sure who made dad angrier—the girls or himself for not checking on them sooner.

For most of the time I lived at home, I thought of Judi and Jenni as my bratty little sisters. They would get me in trouble, mess with my computer, and embarrass me in front of my dates. Because of our age difference, Judi and Jenni only have patchy memories of me living at home. They were eight when I went off to college. They were fourteen when our mother passed. When I went off to seminary, they kind of knew the importance of it, but they were teenagers with their own lives to manage. I lived about two hours away from them while they were navigating their teenage years. So it seemed rather sudden to me when I observed that they had turned into beautiful young women, each seeking her own path. Judi wanted to be a nurse. Jenni wanted to be a teacher.

Jenni was intelligent. She was not only smart; she was beloved. Knowing her meant loving her. Her peers in college loved her, her fellow teachers loved her, and her students loved her. Her ambition was to earn a PhD in education and become the director of the Teaching Fellows program.

Jenni was also a person of great warmth and grace. Once when she was getting treatment at Duke, she came to stay at my house. My oldest daughter, who was just a small girl at the time, wanted to do Jenni's makeup. Jenni stayed still and let a little girl put lipstick all over her. Her face was covered in red lipstick. I don't imagine Jenni felt well that day, but she played with my daughter anyway.

On one of Jenni's prior stays at Duke, I went to see her and brought my daughter along with me. Because of her age, she could not go in to see Jenni. Jenni was aware of the rules and went to the glass door at the end of the hall. There she played with my daughter through the window. My daughter was delighted. I think Jenni was too.

Now this wonderful, bright, compassionate, faithful person was gone. I could not get my mind around the reality of her loss. It was as if one of the bright spots in the universe was extinguished. I had no answers. I hardly knew the right questions to ask. Jenni was gone. I was crushed. I desperately wanted to hear from God, and I heard nothing. The silence was intolerable. I began a descent into darkness that I could not have imagined only a few months before.

CHAPTER 2

Preaching in the Darkness

When I first arrived in Roanoke Rapids, I was invited to preach in a series of Lenten luncheon worship services. These services were an annual affair, hosted by the congregations in the main street area of our community. One of the congregations would host the services, while a pastor from another congregation would preach. The more tenured ministers were happy to have a new person to share in the preaching responsibilities, and I was glad to accept the invitation. I had accepted it weeks before Jenni's passing and before I realized the gravity of Jenni's situation. It was now April 1, 2009, and it was my Wednesday to preach the short homily. It had only been nine days since Jenni's death. In retrospect, I should have politely and apologetically withdrawn. Since I was new to my church and new in town, however, I was trying to make the right impression. I did not want to be seen as someone who breaks commitments. So I followed through. Unfortunately, my raw emotions got the best of me, and I think the gathered believers got more than they bargained for that day.

I strode up to the pulpit at Rosemary United Methodist Church, my church's next-door neighbor, wearing my black robe and purple stole. I looked over the crowd. There were a few familiar faces from my congregation. Bernie, my friend who came to the hospital to visit me, was there along with several members of my congregation. Also in the sanctuary were Methodists, Presbyterians, Lutherans, Episcopalians, and more than a few Catholics. Most of the assembled believers were new to me, but they appeared to have high hopes for the sermon. I was new and young. They perhaps were looking for a youthful, energetic, hopeful sermon. Unfortunately, I had none of those qualities to bring to my preaching that day. I was broken. I began:[4]

> Have you ever noticed the little lies we tell each other just to have something to say? For example, if someone says, "How are you doing?" we say, "Fine." The last thing we want people to do when we ask that question is to answer it. Those who actually do answer it are a little . . . well . . . off. I mean, have you ever asked someone how they were doing and then gotten an answer? "My arthritis is acting up, my bursitis is causing me pain, and don't even talk to me about my diverticulitis." The first thing you want to do is to get away from that conversation as quickly as possible. We do not really want the unvarnished truth. We just want the little lies that make conversation normal.
>
> We even tell these little lies at funerals. Have you ever heard a conversation between two people who are looking at a casket that sounded like this: "Look at her. Doesn't she look so good"? No, she doesn't look good. She's dead. Dead people do not look good, and if they did look good, what does that say about how they looked when they were living? No, we tell little lies.
>
> Today, I'm going to side with the oddballs. If you ask me how I am doing, I will tell you the truth. I am disappointed with God.

Just a few days ago I lost my sister, Jenni, one of the most amazing people I have ever known. Jenni was remarkable in every way, and after a long stay at Duke, she is gone.

I am disappointed with God because I thought God would intervene. For the record, I was not asking for the skies to split and a massive miracle to occur. I was simply wanting God to help the ordinary treatments to work. God did not intervene.

I want you to think of the great promises of prayer. John 14:13 reads, "And I will do whatever you ask in my name so that the Father may be glorified in the Son." Matthew 21:22 reads, "And all things you ask in prayer, believing, you will receive." John 15:7 reads, "If you abide in me, and my words abide in you, ask whatever you wish, and it will be done for you."

What is one to make of the distance between the claims the Scriptures make about prayer and our actual lives? What are we to say when a loved one is sick and does not get better? In the case of my sister, over 10,000 people from around the world were praying for her. I suppose one could argue that a single individual's prayers were defective. I suppose one could say that a single individual had unconfessed sin or a lack of faith. Maybe. On the other hand, I find it unlikely that among 10,000 people, there would not be a single person with enough faith or enough faithful practice to pray correctly. I also would have thought that the sheer number of people praying would itself be enough. In other words, I have a hard time believing that all the prayers on Jenni's behalf were defective individually or collectively. So I have no choice. Since I cannot conclude that the prayers were defective, I must conclude that God did not choose to help my sister, promises about prayer in the New Testament notwithstanding.

Romans 8 teaches us that God will cause all things to come together for the good for those who are in Christ. I do struggle to see the good today. I struggle to see how good comes out of lives that are cut short. I do not see good. Rather, I see harm everywhere. Perhaps someday, when enough time has passed, I might see the good. Today is a different matter.

So that leaves me with a problem. How am I supposed to think about God now? How am I supposed to trust him? If I cannot trust him with my sister's life, how can I trust him on eternal matters? How can I trust him with my prayers in the future? I wish I had a good answer. I do not. I comfort myself with the fact that I am not the first person to ask the question.

Psalm 44 is listed as a Psalm of Lament. It is a complaint. In truth there are many Psalms of Lament. When we think of Psalms we often think of the great Psalms of Praise: "O LORD, our LORD, how excellent is Your name in all the earth . . ." or "The heavens declare the glory of God . . ." or "Make a joyful noise unto the LORD, all ye lands. Serve the LORD with gladness. Come into his presence with singing." While the full-throated praises of these psalms are an important part of the Psalter, God gave us the Lament Psalms too, for not everything feels praiseworthy.

Interestingly, Psalm 44 is not a complaint about the psalmist's enemies. The psalms are full of those. Often a psalm will recount the ways of the wicked and implore God to act. Often a psalm will complain to God about the psalmist's enemies and ask for God to intervene. This psalm is different. The complaint is not about the wicked, or national enemies, or personal enemies, or events in general. This psalm is a complaint *about God* directed *toward God*.

Psalm 44 begins by recounting the mighty works of God. It was God who drove out the nations before Israel. It was God who provided military victory for the armies of Israel, and the people knew it. They knew that God's protection and provision was what had provided them a home and shielded it from their enemies. For eight verses, the psalmist speaks of the victories of God. Then the unnamed writer boasts in God and praises God's name. "We will praise your name forever," he writes.

Then the psalm turns. Suddenly the psalmist changes tone. He writes, "But you have rejected and humiliated us; you do not march out with our armies." The Lord, the Great Shepherd of Psalm 23, is now the Lord who hands over his people to be "eaten like sheep." He has not protected them like the Good Shepherd of Psalm 23; he has scattered them like an assailant. He has not given them honor. He has made them a laughingstock and a joke. The Lord has covered them in shame. The psalmist's accusations against God are striking.

Normally, the writers of the Old Testament see themselves as the problem. If there was a calamity, then it was caused by God as a punishment for the sin of the people. There was a clear-cut line between obedience to the covenant and the fate of the nation. Failure to keep the covenant yielded doom. This psalm, however, does not see it that way. The writer utterly denies that the people had worshiped foreign gods. He claims that since God knows the secrets of the heart, then God would have seen any disobedience. The people were being killed, and the writer pointedly says it was God's fault. "Because of you we are slain all day long." The crisis was God's doing, and the psalmist was reaching out to God for help.

I wonder if you have felt this way before. I wonder if you have been disappointed with God. I wonder if you look at your situation and think that if God were the God he claims to be, then the world would be different—your life would be different.

What are we to do when we feel this way? Should we run away from God? In our anger and shock, are we to conclude that the faith is not worth keeping? I am reminded of something Peter said in John 6. Jesus' teachings had finally scandalized his followers. Jesus had told them that those who eat his flesh and drink his blood have eternal life. Jesus' followers were taken aback. The shock is hard for us to imagine. When we hear these words, the first thing we naturally think of is Communion as the body and blood of Christ. Jesus' first followers did not have this history yet. How in the world would they have understood his words? They were shocked and deeply disturbed. Realizing his followers' reaction, Jesus asked what they would do if they saw Jesus ascend into heaven. Now Jesus was making a claim to be divine, further shocking his followers. The reaction was predictable: people ceased following Jesus. In what looks to be a very sad moment, Jesus said, "You do not want to leave too, do you?" Peter responded, "Lord, to whom shall we go? You have the words of eternal life." I share that thought with Peter. To leave the faith is an act of futility. The words of life come from Jesus. Eternal life comes from Jesus. Everything that is true and good comes from Jesus. Everything I have and hold to comes from Jesus. Running away is not an option. Telling the truth, however, is.

So I believe something about God. I believe God is big enough to handle the truth today. I believe God is able to handle the truth about me and you. I believe God is big enough to know the truth about where my heart is, and I believe he wants to hear from me. I believe he gave us the Lament Psalms as an example of how to pray. Not all prayers are celebrations of the ways of God. Sometimes, prayer is a complaint *to God about God*.

The reason we get a psalm like Psalm 44 is that it serves as an example. The feelings we have about God must be spoken to God. To avoid that is to avoid healing. We cannot bury our sadness with empty platitudes or shallow slogans. To heal we must tell the truth. More specifically, we must tell the truth to God.

As I said, I should have politely turned down the invitation to preach that day. The preceding weeks had been brutal on my soul. The sweet people who heard my sermon had to be scandalized. My friend from Rosemary who was in attendance, Bernie, said there were a few audible gasps in the sanctuary. I half-jokingly thought the community might conclude that I was some sort of heretic. My feelings were raw, I was wounded to the deepest part of my soul, and I did not try to hide that fact.

Saying those words was a bit cathartic, though. I was able to breathe a little easier. The reception of my sermon was not as bad as I thought it would be. While some were taken aback, especially at the beginning, the gathered believers understood why I preached the way I did that day.

As it turns out, most people have a spiritual wound. As New Testament scholar Thomas Long writes, "everyone has a quarrel with God."[5] Having just come to my new church, I had no way of knowing the stories of my members' lives at that point, but many of them had deep spiritual wounds also. One of the deacons in my church had buried two wives. One of our members had a child drown while in the care of a friend. Some of our members had suffered late-term miscarriages. Another family had buried one daughter by the time I arrived and would soon bury another. I was wounded, but I was not alone in being wounded. Many of them had felt, and were still feeling, the raw emotion I expressed.

Valid Questions

While I was in no emotional or spiritual condition to be preaching, the questions I raised were absolutely valid. The Bible *is* full of wonderful promises about prayer. We *are* promised that God will hear us when we pray. We *are* promised that God will act on our behalf. We *are* invited to come to God for our daily needs. Further, we have good reasons to expect that God will meet those needs. It is promised:

"And my God will meet all of your needs according to his riches in glory in Christ Jesus" (Phil 4:19); "Ask, and it will be given to you; seek, and you will find; knock, and the door will be opened for you. For everyone who asks receives; the one who seeks finds; for the one who knocks, the door will be opened" (Matt 7:7-8).

So what was I to make of the fact that God did not intervene in Jenni's case? Two things were at issue for me. The first was the reliability of Scripture and the second was the character of God. It came down to a simple question: In light of these events, could I trust God's character and what the Scriptures say about God? My trust in God was also broken because of a sense I had before losing Jenni. When Jenni was preparing for her stem cell transplant, I prayed about her constantly. Following all of my prayers, I had a deep sense of peace. I believed the sense of peace meant that Jenni would be okay. When she was not okay, it felt like a betrayal. When neither ordinary recovery or healing took place, what was I to conclude?

Many contemporary believers, especially in the Reformed tradition, have concluded that the age of miracles has ended. The end of the Apostolic age brought an end to the miraculous signs that accompanied the first preaching of the gospel. In one respect, it would be emotionally and intellectually easier to agree with them. If God does not do the miraculous anymore, then I cannot blame God for not doing one in this case. I, however, cannot agree with the idea that God's miraculous activity has completely ceased. The witness of the people of God throughout the ages, the witness of the people of God throughout the world, and the witness of the Scriptures do not point to God ceasing miraculous activity. No, God is still the God of power and wonder. Miracles still happen. They just did not happen for Jenni.

Glib Answers

If my questions seemed unanswerable, that did not stop many people from trying to answer them. As a quirk of my personality, I loathe clichés. They make my skin crawl. When clichés appear in the spiritual life, I find them particularly repugnant. Ordinarily, clichés are just bad habits of speech. In the spiritual life, however, they can do actual harm.

My dislike for the phrase "God needed another angel" has a long history, but in the aftermath of Jenni's death my dislike of it became intense. This common phrase, intended to give comfort, is so full of mischief that it should never be spoken. First, God has no need. God is the unlimited, omnipotent, infinite sustainer of all that exists. God is completely perfect in God's nature. God creates not out of need but out of the eternal bliss of God's being. To suggest that God has a need is to make ourselves adhere to a lesser "god." Second, the Christian faith has never taught that believers become angels when we die. We may have similar characteristics in the life to come, but angels are angels and people are people. Third, if God wanted another angel, God would not have to "take" a person. God would only need to create another angel.

I also learned to have a deepened disdain for the statement "God will never give you more than you can handle." Nothing in the Scriptures intimates such an idea. The cliché comes from a passage about temptation in 1 Corinthians 10:13: "God is faithful, and he will not let you be tempted beyond what you are able, but with the temptation he will also provide a way of escape that you may be able to endure it." The passage is not about the difficulties we face in life but about the temptations we face. By the way, God is never the tempter. Further, taken at face value, the cliché gives us reason to remain weak and immature. If by doing so we experience fewer difficult events, why not be as weak as possible? Worse still, the phrase points us away from the scriptural truth that God is our sustainer when we are week. We should not rest in the idea that God will not give us anything that we cannot handle. We should rest in the idea that God is our helper and fortress no matter what we face. We may face things that we have no idea how to handle. There is no difficulty, however, that God cannot handle.

I really learned to hate the cliché "It was God's will." What kind of God wills death for a young person? What kind of God would will the death of those who follow him? Does this not make God into a petty tyrant? Perhaps in the cold light of distance, one could ponder the mystery of God's will and human suffering. In the light of the death of a loved one, however, this statement provides no comfort at all. If the statement were true, it would actually provide reasons to rage all the more at the God who caused death.

I simply refused to be comforted by the glib clichés offered by well-meaning believers. I wanted something deeper. I needed real answers with real heft. I found few, and I was not going to get answers any time soon.

CHAPTER 3

The Descent Spirals

If losing Jenni were the sum of my losses, it would have been bad enough. Losing her, however, was just the beginning of my descent into darkness. In May 2009, a few weeks after Jenni died, I started to have a persistently scratchy throat and my voice became raspy. I remember staring aimlessly out of the car window when I finally gave voice to the fear that my voice was becoming a problem.

It was not the first time my voice had become problematic. In June 2008, I was singing during worship when my voice failed. After the hymns, when it was time to preach, my voice was gone. A member of the congregation, someone very dear to me, realized something was wrong and quickly brought me a cup of water. After drinking, I managed to speak, but it was not my normal voice. It was weak and raspy. I sounded like an odd combination of Bill Clinton and Mickey Mouse. It was like I had suddenly developed a throat infection. Because the first symptom of Jenni's cancer was losing her voice, I became frightened—terrified, to be honest. I feared the worst. I scheduled a doctor's appointment as quickly as possible. My primary care physician, Dr. Maria Fakadej, got me in fairly quickly, but she was unable to get a good look at my voice box. Realizing my family history, Dr. Fakadej quickly forwarded me to Dr. Spector, an ear, nose, and throat (ENT) specialist.

The wait between seeing my primary doctor and seeing the specialist was difficult. The mind can create all kinds of possibilities and alternative realities when it has no explanation for what is really going on. Finally, the day of my appointment arrived. Dr. Spector had an excellent reputation and was more like a slightly disheveled medical scientist than a doctor in both his appearance and demeanor. He slouched, his dirty blond hair was never quite in place, and his glasses looked to be a few years out of fashion. His shoulders would hunch forward as he looked to the ground, paced, and stroked his chin while explaining medical realities. After taking one look into my throat, he said there was a growth on the flap above my voice box that was making it difficult for the flap to operate correctly. The growth was impeding my natural speech patterns; it was the source of my problem. Naturally, with Jenni's history, I had to ask if the growth was cancerous. The doctor's flat demeanor and scholarly affect were comforting. No, it was not cancer. It was scar tissue. The tissue was probably caused by overuse of my voice or by acid reflux. In either case, the treatment began with voice rest. The entire Wallace clan was relieved.

For one month, I was not allowed to speak. The hope was that the tissue would heal on its own given enough rest. For the first few days, I was reduced to making hand gestures to get my point across, but then I got a dry erase board so I could write what I needed to say. As a person who uses speech to make a living, it was interesting not being able to speak words at all. It was also interesting trying to lead a church without being able to speak. I had to get guest ministers to preach in my stead, and I had to find ways to lead my congregation without my voice. It was a challenge.

It was also a challenge because I had a small child at home at the time. She was not quite three. For an almost three-year-old, it is difficult to understand why Daddy suddenly cannot talk. Listening to her trying to explain that she was upset because I did not talk to her was the worst part of the voice rest. I would hug her, hold her, and let her know I loved her as best I could without words. In the end, however, I would sometimes break down and talk.

The month passed as slowly as the Carolina humidity, but when it did, I visited with Dr. Spector again. The news was not good. The growth had not shrunk at all, and Dr. Spector recommended surgery. Agreeing with him, I scheduled the procedure for December 2008. The surgery went well, but I required a week of voice rest afterward. After going through one month of voice rest, one week seemed easy. Dr. Spector believed the surgery would be effective and that no further medical intervention would be necessary. January 2009 was supposed to be the end of my voice issues. It was not.

In May 2009, still reeling from Jenni's loss, I found my voice getting scratchy again. At first, I wondered if it were allergies or even a spring cold, but it was too persistent. The feeling was familiar. At first, I did not even want to say it. Finally, though, it was unavoidable. The growth was back.

Now living in Roanoke Rapids, I reached out to Dr. Spector again. This time, he took on a more ominous demeanor. These kinds of growths, he argued, are usually mitigated with surgery. Frankly, he was surprised that the growth had come back at all. To come back and be large enough to cause medical issues was significant. This time he not only scheduled surgery but also put me on two medications. The first was for acid reflux. The other medication, baclofen, was for spasms in my esophagus. Dr. Spector believed that while I was not experiencing symptoms of acid reflux, I could have been having spasms that threw acid on my voice box, causing the scar tissue, even though I was unaware. In fact, he was fairly certain acid reflux was my problem. The treatment plan seemed reasonable to me, and we scheduled the second surgery.

Surgery was successful. In a few weeks I was back to normal. The good results only lasted a few months, however. The scar tissue returned again. This time Dr. Spector got very concerned. I did as well. Since we had not prevented the growth from recurring, it seemed that either the diagnosis or the treatment plan was faulty. The standard of care for such growths was voice rest, medicine for acid reflux, and surgery, and none of this was working. In another six months I was back for a third surgery. I was starting to wonder if I would have to quit being a minister.

After the growth reemerged for the fourth time, Dr. Spector concluded that I needed to have a different perspective on my throat, so he forwarded me to a doctor at the University of North Carolina ENT Clinic, Dr. Robert Buckmire. Dr. Buckmire's credentials were exceptional, and he was renowned for his expertise in treating voice issues. He did not believe that the cause of my issue was acid reflux. He believed the problem was in the way I used my voice. After surgery, he injected Botox into my voice box. The Botox had the effect of temporarily causing me to be unable to speak. The plan was to force my voice to rest for healing. Then, as I recovered, I was to undergo voice training to relearn how to speak. Dr. Buckmire believed that his plan would bring an end to my issues.

Dr. Buckmire had an in-house speech pathologist whom I visited regularly for speech lessons. As the Botox wore off over a number of weeks, I visited the speech pathologist and learned how to speak correctly. I learned how to breathe properly when speaking. I learned to enunciate correctly. I did lots of odd exercises and retrained my speech. The plan was in full swing.

The plan failed. Growths continued to emerge more quickly than before. At first, I needed to have surgery every six months. By this point, I needed surgery every four months. In other words, the time from the end of post-surgery voice rest until the point my symptoms reemerged was around ten weeks.

New Symptoms

Slowly, I started developing a new symptom: pain. The pain would typically come in the middle of the day, originating in my knees. Knee pain was not new to me. Even as a teenager I suffered from pain in my knees. In fact, when I was sixteen I tore cartilage in my right knee and had arthroscopic surgery. With that history, I just assumed the pain was from my youthful participation in sports. I thought I was dealing with arthritis, but the pain kept getting worse. It amazes me how slowly and imperceptibly the pain increased. At first it was just an ache. Then it was an ache that could not be treated with over-the-counter medications. Then the pain kept me still, as moving was uncomfortable. After several weeks, being still was no longer an option. The pain would not allow it. I could not be still at all, and I used warmth to help. Some of my church members noticed that I kept putting a blazer in my lap to keep my legs warm. They and the children they ministered with bought me an afghan with the Lord's Prayer on it. The church staff started to call me Grandpa. I felt like a grandpa; I moved like a grandpa, and I was not yet forty years old. I was simply debilitated. At the peak of the pain, I had to go home from work at lunch and get under a blanket so the warmth could keep the pain at bay, at least temporarily. Eventually, I developed a new symptom along with the pain—chronic muscle spasms. I consulted with doctors, but I got nowhere. I suspect that once they ruled out structural issues, they did not investigate further. Perhaps they thought I was trying to get prescription pain medicine. I was resigned to the idea that the pain would be part of my life.

The pain had another effect. I could not rest. I developed a profound sleep disorder. The nights I got more than a few hours of rest were rare. Maybe every ten days I got a semblance of a good night's sleep. The problem was that I could not be still. I would toss and turn for hours. I found myself trying to go to bed earlier and earlier, not so much because I needed the sleep but because it took me hours to find a way to be still. Simply put, I was a mess.

Of course, the lack of sleep left me groggy during the day. The worst days were when I had to travel. Because Roanoke Rapids is fairly small and isolated, many of our members would travel to Raleigh, North Carolina, or Richmond, Virginia, for medical care—especially if they had a major issue. As their pastor, I made a point to visit with them. Being groggy, though, made the three-hour round trips to Raleigh or Richmond very hard. I chose to eat to stay awake, and I had to eat a lot. Predictably, my health suffered. My weight ballooned. As a young man, I was very active and athletic. I usually thought of myself as too skinny. When I graduated college, I weighed in at 150 pounds. For a 5-foot-10 man, that is very thin. By now, I had shot up to over 215. Worse, my body chemistry was going haywire, and my cholesterol went through the roof. The doctors wanted me to go on a statin, but the statin increased my pain so much that I could not take it. I was a medical emergency waiting for a place to happen.

The throat issues were unrelenting. Speech therapy was ineffective, as was the Botox, as was the surgery. Nothing kept the growths from returning. The doctors and I began to consider radical alternatives. Moving back to the original diagnosis of acid reflux, we began to consider doing a procedure called the Nissen fundoplication or Nissen loop. Essentially, the procedure creates a valve by turning the stomach on itself. The intended result is that nothing would come back up out of the stomach into the esophagus. It would eliminate any problems with acid reflux. It is a serious procedure, however, and I did not take the idea lightly.

Marital Stress

On top of this, my marriage was in deep trouble. I had known from some time that things had become difficult. I had married in the last semester of my senior year of college, sixteen years previously. As with any marriage, we had been through many ups and downs. From the months preceding the move to Rosemary until this point, the marriage had been in repeated crisis and terrifying ordeals. On top of losing Jenni and dealing with my health issues, we had financial worries. We had not been able to sell our house where we lived while I served my previous church. The house was 1.5 hours away from our new home in Roanoke Rapids. The situation seemed untenable, and there was no ready solution.

Then a short crisis emerged. My daughter needed to have her adenoids removed, and some preliminary tests were done for her including imaging. The doctor spotted a cyst on her brain. Naturally, I was terrified. I immediately sought out a pediatric neurologist who diagnosed the cyst as the result of a perinatal stroke. She was young enough, he stated, that her brain had compensated. She was to going to be fine, he said. She just had to avoid brain injury at all costs. That news, while a relief, set me to constant worrying about her.

In the time I had been at Rosemary Baptist, I had been through crisis after crisis. They took their toll on my marriage. Finally, in 2011 my then-wife left. She took our daughter and moved back into our old house ninety minutes away. After twenty-four hours, she thought through it and invited me to live in the old house, but she was not going back to Roanoke Rapids. I moved back into our old home, but I did so knowing there was little hope for our marriage. The situation was grim. In addition to all the other issues, I now had a three-hour daily commute and a loving church that did not like that I was no longer living in the community.

The Crash

Because of how I perceived her behavior, I concluded that talking with my former wife about my medical condition was impossible. From my perspective, her anxiety was so strong that it made having a serious discussion about any important issue unhelpful. I was going to have to figure my health issues out on my own. I had my sixth surgery on my throat and then my seventh. I was in despair.

Dr. Buckmire finally decided that he could not help me anymore. He did have a word of insight that changed everything for me, though. He said that the cause of the first growth may always be unknown, but the *surgeries themselves* were causing the subsequent growths. He then forwarded me to Dr. Seth Cohen of Duke.

Dr. Cohen had a revolutionary treatment that used a fiber optic cord and a laser to kill growths like mine. I thought it had to be better than what I was going through. The procedure was outpatient. There was no general anesthesia. At least the cost and downtime had to be better, even if it yielded the same results. I had an appointment on the calendar. Finally, I had a breakthrough, but there was yet another breakdown first.

In the days prior to my visit with Dr. Cohen, I was in the walk-in closet getting some clothes when, suddenly, I sneezed. When I did, every muscle in my torso spasmed at once. I collapsed. I was not quite forty years old, and I was a heap of flesh on the closet floor. I have come to think of this moment as a symbol of where I was in my life. I was ruined spiritually, emotionally, and physically. For those moments when I was collapsed on the tan carpet, I realized this was not life. This was a living death.

The Bible talks about the struggle between light and darkness, good and evil. In those moments while I was a broken man in a heap of flesh on the closet floor, it felt like darkness had won. I realized that if I were going to live, life would have to be very different. The collapse was the moment when everything changed for me. It was the moment I decided to take charge of my life and live again. That moment, I was a pile of flesh on the floor. I was sick. I was tired. I was depressed. My marriage was practically over. I thought I might lose my job when the inevitable divorce occurred. I was afraid of losing my daughter. I was grieving my sister. I was in pain. Frankly, I was miserable. Somehow, in God's grace, I found the resolve to get up. I found the will to *live*.

Still terrified of my condition due to the collapse, I consulted Google. Google is excellent at many things, but it is a terrible doctor. The articles my Google search produced convinced me I had multiple sclerosis. I scheduled an appointment with another doctor for a consultation. Before I could get to my appointment, a moment of grace happened. I ran out of baclofen, the muscle relaxer I was taking to prevent the esophageal spasms. It dawned on me that if Dr. Buckmire was right with his assertion about surgery being the cause of my growths, then I did not need to take this medication. So I did not refill the prescription. My body's response was shocking and almost immediate. Within forty-eight hours, my body started to change. I was suddenly in less pain. The cramps dissipated. I felt dramatically better. To my horror, I discovered that many of my symptoms were a negative side effect of baclofen. The medicine I was taking to save my voice was, quite literally, poisoning me. I was mortified and relieved at the same time.

A Reprieve and a Divorce

Shortly thereafter, I had my first appointment with Dr. Cohen. His procedure put an end to my voice issues. Before seeing him, I had seven surgeries on my throat. After having two outpatient procedures with him, my problems ceased. I have never had an issue since. My longsuffering congregation erupted in applause at the news. Finally, I was past all of my voice issues, and I was getting better.

My marriage was not getting better, however. On the contrary, it was getting much, much worse. Counseling was not helpful, and the fighting intensified. More difficult than the fighting was the frosty silence. Some marriages die with explosive fighting. Ours died in a frigid arctic blast of silence. By the time the fighting emerged, it was too late. In January 2013, we separated for the final time.

On the day the final separation happened, I began to inform my congregation. I reasoned that if many members of the congregation requested it, I would turn in my resignation. With my mind reeling from all of the possible bad scenarios, I prepared my answer for what was happening. I started sharing the news in the weekly staff meeting. There I told our music minister, youth director, and secretary the news. I did not know what to expect. I told them there was the possibility that I would need to resign. While they were aware it could happen, they were confident the church would not require it.

After the staff meeting, I went to talk to the core leaders of the church one at a time. I shared the story as many times as I could until the repetition became too much to bear. After many conversations and several hours, I went home. It was cold and dark. As I reflected on the difficult day, I noted that no one had asked me to leave. I was surprised. They were willing to love me and have me be their pastor even through this nightmare. They were—and are—a wonderful congregation. What also struck me was that virtually no one was surprised. Only once did I hear, "I cannot believe it." While I thought the struggles in my marriage were private, nearly everyone already knew. The smile I wore like an ill-fitting Sunday shoe fooled absolutely no one. I was in a deep struggle, and everyone knew it.

Losses and Faith

I had to negotiate my struggle through my anger. I was angry, livid, at God. I held it personally against God that Jenni was gone. Oddly enough, the rest of the crises did not have the same effect on me. They were hard, yes, but the faith-shaking crisis was Jenni's death. My sister was gone, and I was determined *not* to get past it. I know it makes no sense, but I was holding a grudge against God. I know it is silly, even heretical, to suggest that I had to forgive God. In truth, God has been so good to me that I should only ever respond in profound gratitude. Even if I had to suffer horribly for the rest of my days, God would only deserve praise from me. In the middle of my crises, though, I could not see that. I was holding a grudge against God that I was determined to take to the grave. I planned to go to the throne of God and demand an explanation. Worse, it seemed like failing to hold the grudge was tantamount to betraying Jenni. If I let go, I was not fighting for the honor and dignity of this amazing woman. It felt morally wrong to let go. None of that has theological support, but as a man in deep grief, it was how I felt.

Of course, as one who was angry with God, prayer became very hard for me. I did not stop praying, but my prayers became difficult. I felt unsure about prayers that asked God to intervene in human affairs. I was fine with asking for forgiveness. I regularly asked for direction. Prayers for God's intervention, though, stopped making sense. I wondered, "God will do whatever God knows to be right, so what point is there in asking anyway?"

Worse, my emotional state played out in public. When you are a pastor, there is no place to hide your relationship with God. You are sharing publicly every week. My sermons became technical. The arid, scholarly side of my personality dominated, but it did so with an air of anger and condescension. Obviously, my sermons were not in any sense effective. They were as dead as I was.

Responding to Crises

For many people, life crises turn into crises of faith. For me, I never stopped believing. That is not to suggest an absence of spiritual struggle. Quite the contrary—it was a profound struggle. The darkness was overwhelming. The struggle was brutal. My struggle, though, was not about God's *existence* but about God's *character*. I struggled with exactly how God governed the world and what God's character was really like. In some respects, I am still working that out. I am settled with God's goodness, but I do struggle with how God manages the affairs of earth. I do wonder about how God's sovereignty works. While I have come to some conclusions, I suspect I will ponder the mystery of God's sovereignty for the rest of my days. I am okay with ambiguity, although that is a recent development. I have decided I do not need to have all the answers. I do need God.

I do not think of myself as particularly virtuous because I remained faithful. In truth, the faith held a much better grip on me than I ever held on it. In those dark winter days of my soul, I had to process a lot. When a person goes through a divorce, there is a profound renegotiation of identity. Because of the fusion of identity that happens in marriage, it becomes hard to know yourself without your spouse. It is especially hard to know yourself without your spouse after sixteen years. I had to figure out me again. That was difficult. Recovering from my sickness, grieving for Jenni, and pondering my divorce all while being a pastor was emotionally draining. There were days when I was just lost. There were days when everything was up for grabs. There were many, many dark days. Even during those worst moments, however, God held on to me. My faith held on to me.

Yes, I did choose to remain faithful. There were multiple points along the way when I could have walked away. One of the great mysteries of the faith is the connection between Divine initiative and human response. I tend to believe God's initiative empowers human response. I believe Christ is the one who has saved us and the one who will keep us. I also know that, somehow, some way, I did not want to lose my faith.

It was not because of any special ability or insight on my part that I survived. It was not because I have anything special about my character that I held on to my faith. God saved me. God saved me when I was a little kid, and God kept me when everything in my life fell apart. When I was angry at God, God loved me. When I would not be comforted, God kept me. Even though there was a long period of time when I didn't want it, God healed me. To the extent that I am healed, it is not because I am good. It is because God is good.

CHAPTER 4

Nothingness

Among the positively nerdy things I do is watch TED Talks. For those who do not speak nerd, TED Talks are talks given by experts in a variety of fields. Even though I find them very interesting, most of the tech talks are outside my bailiwick. Many focus on science and technology, success and self-improvement, and other techy kinds of subjects. I stumbled across one, however, that was directly in my field of knowledge—theology and the problem of evil. It was by Kate Bowler, a professor at Duke Divinity School. I was interested immediately. Dr. Bowler had been diagnosed with stage IV colon cancer, a diagnosis that is usually terminal. In heartbreaking detail, she describes her desire to live and her questions about God. She said, "I want to live long enough to embarrass my son," who was then only a small child. "I want to live long enough to see my husband's beautiful hair fall out." She not only had a vague desire to live; she was fighting every day for survival. She found herself in a clinical trial that was giving her time. The treatments required her to fly to Atlanta every week. Flying weekly to Atlanta to get treatment was exhausting, but for a chance at life, it was worth it. She thought maybe, just maybe, she would get to live.

Her story, of course, struck me. What struck me just as much was something she said about the experience of maybe dying. What she felt was love. In her book *Everything Happens for a Reason and Other Lies I've Loved* she put it this way:

> In those first few days after my diagnosis, when I was in the hospital, I couldn't see my son, I couldn't get out of bed, and I couldn't say for certain that I would survive the year. But I felt as though I'd uncovered something like a secret about faith. Even in lucid moments I found my feeling so difficult to explain. I kept saying the same thing: "I don't want to go back; I don't want to go back."
>
> At the time when I should have felt abandoned by God, I was not reduced to ashes. . . . The feeling stayed with me for months. In fact, I had grown so accustomed to that floating feeling that I started to panic at the prospect of losing it.[6]

The feeling was love. Reading Dr. Bowler describe it in her book was moving. Seeing her TED Talk, however, was life changing for me. She describes a feeling that was totally missing when I descended into darkness.

It was a feeling I longed for and did not have, and it was not the first time. I had wanted it and been without it earlier. In the winter of 1997, I received a call that I had dreaded for months. My mother had taken a turn for the worse. Mom had fought against breast cancer for several years, and it was not going well. She complained rarely, but the grimace on her face as she walked gave away what was going on inside. The treatments were not helping. The cancer was not receding. Worse, she was in constant pain. The family asked if she needed to stop working, and my mom said no. "If I stop working, that's it." She refused to give up, and quitting work felt like giving up. This turn for the worse was not as sudden for others as it seemed to me, living two hours away. I got the call while I was traveling, and once the shock passed

I went to the Bennettsville, South Carolina, hospital where Mom was being treated. Mom had been a social worker at the hospital for many years, and when she was ill they took excellent care of her. When I arrived, the entire family had already gathered in an ominous assembly. Things were grim, and we knew it. The hospital was good to us; there was an entire empty hall in the hospital where we were allowed to gather, pray, and wait. The people from our home church came as well. They filled the hall with their presence and love. They were very kind. There were many of them, and they stayed. For hours they visited us in the hospital hallway and in the room, but despite their presence, I felt alone.

As the hours passed, our guests left and only the family and our dearest friends remained. I believe it was after midnight when my dad, my dad's lifelong friend Danny, and I were in the room with Mom. Dad and Danny began to pray, and something happened. It is something I do not really have words for. Suddenly, the prayers turned to shouts. They were not shouts of anger or fear. They were not even shouts of desperation. For Dad and Danny, the joy of the Lord was in the room. I witnessed the event, confused and a little jealous. Hours earlier, I had pulled a chair beside the bed, started holding my mother's hand, and rested my forehead on the edge of the hospital mattress. While Dad and Danny were enraptured with the glory of God, I observed them and felt nothing. I simply held Mom's hand with my head down, trying not to fall apart. When Dad and Danny were experiencing the presence of God in an utterly amazing way, I felt nothing but deep sorrow.

There are many people who have experienced what Dr. Bowler has described. Great saints of church history report it. Many saints of lesser renown have experienced it too.

One of my mentors in ministry tells a story about a family in his church. They had a small girl who was born very sick. For weeks after her birth, she was in and out of the hospital. As the trips to the hospital grew more frequent, the hope of her survival grew more remote. One Sunday morning as my friend was in his office preparing for worship, he got a call. "Our little girl is gone." My friend went over to the house immediately and prayed with the family. After the prayer, the father of the little girl said, "Sometime, I want to tell people what has happened, because I feel God's presence now in a way I never have before."

I wanted to have that kind of experience. I did not. I experienced nothing. I just remember how dark the night my mom's death was. I also remember that in the darkness of that night, I felt alone.

Much the same happened after the loss of Jenni. I was sitting in the same position, in a chair beside the bed, holding her hand, resting my forehead on the hospital mattress. As Jenni's breaths slowed, I would have loved to have experienced what Dr. Bowler talked about. I would have loved to know God's presence in the way my friend's parishioner did. I did not.

I do note that C. S. Lewis experienced the same absence. In his masterpiece, *A Grief Observed*, Lewis also reckons with the seeming absence of God in his hour of deepest need. He writes,

> Meanwhile, where is God? This is one of the most disquieting symptoms. When you are happy, so happy that you have no sense of needing Him, so happy that you are tempted to feel His claims upon you as an interruption, if you remember yourself and turn to him with gratitude and praise, you will be—or so it feels—welcomed with opened arms. But go to him when your need

is desperate, when all other help is vain, and what do
you find? A door slammed in your face, and the sound
of bolting and double bolting on the inside. After that,
silence.[7]

I deeply longed for God's presence, but whatever presence
I felt was too subtle to notice. I rather like to think that
God's presence was a sustaining power holding me up even
as I was unaware. Honestly, though, saying that is an act
of faith. I do trust and believe that God sustained me. But
I never felt it.

It is not that I do not know God's presence. I have felt it
often. Many years ago, when I was a college freshman, I was
having a crisis of faith. One night my friends and I gathered
in the sanctuary of the church that was nestled on one corner
of campus and always unlocked. We prayed in the dark
sanctuary until the wee hours of the morning, until God
lifted my spirits with God's Spirit. I have also experienced it
during the times when I have found unusual strength to lead
congregations during crises and when I had to minister to
others who were having their deepest heartbreaks.

I have never, however, found it to be routine. Most of
the time God does not interact with me with definitive
moments of presence. Most of the time with me, God is very
quiet. I'm okay with that. I can be very quiet too. I'm aware
that God is with me in mostly the same way I am aware of
the air. Only when I pay careful attention do I recognize it.
That is, unless the wind is moving powerfully.

As much as I would have liked God to be different with
me than God was during the descent into darkness, it would
have been out of God's character in dealing with me. Why
would the God who meets me in the still quiet suddenly
write flaming messages in the sky? I still wanted it, though.

To be fair, had I actually experienced God's presence when Jenni died, it would have been unpleasant. I was much too angry to experience love. Perhaps that explains the absence of the feeling Dr. Bowler had as much as anything else.

What I have learned is that God refuses to be God in the way I want God to be God. If I were God, I would smite God's enemies and end world hunger. I would give an intrepid researcher the cure to cancer. I would end oppression and persecution. I would bankrupt children's hospitals because I would heal all of their clients. If I were God, no young person would get sick, no old person would suffer, no relationships would be torn. Every good, right, and true desire would come true. If I were God, Jenni would not have died.

I am not God, however. The great theologian of the last century, Karl Barth, was fond of saying, "God is God." It sounds trite until you realize what he means. God, the God of the universe, is God. God alone has the sole right to rule, and God rules according to God's will. Further, I do not have the right to judge God, because I am a feeble human. Even if I were not a mere human, even if I were immortal, endowed with immense power, I would have no standing to judge God. There is no circumstance real or imaginable where I would have the right to judge God. God is still God. And I am not.

There are essentially two wishes we have when it comes to God. The first is that God will do what we think God ought to do. When we have a list of things that God should do, a list of ways God should behave, we end up noticing that seldom does God act in accordance to our will. When God does not, we often go into a semi-pagan practice of trying to manipulate God. Those who offer to us this semi-pagan practice often do so in the guise of Christian teaching. "Say this prayer and God will heal." "Get rid of this sinful practice and God will bless you with good health and prosperity." These promises are not true. If God could be controlled, God would not be God; God would be a genie. Prayers would not be prayers; they would be spells. We would not be faithful followers; we would be shamans. The Bible does teach us to pray, to seek God's face, to come to God with our needs. It does not teach us that if we take certain steps, God will do what we wish. God is not to be trifled with in that way. Those who think God can be manipulated are making God in their own image, after their own likeness. In other words, our lists of how God should govern the world run the risk of idolatry.

The second wish is similar to the first. Wanting God to be God the way we want God to be God is very close to the desire to be God. In reading the Genesis narrative of the fall, one cannot help but notice the substance of the temptation the serpent presented. It was to be like God. Many who read the narrative conclude that human pride manifesting itself in the desire to be God-like, the desire to be God, caused the fall. The fall is the ultimate cause of alienation from God. Pride, therefore, caused the downfall of humanity. Therefore, one should tread carefully with any desire to manage the affairs of God.

It is hard to let God be God when God does not behave the way we want God to behave. It is an act of faith, then, to trust God to be good when everything feels so very, very bad. As hard as it is, it is what is required of us. It is what is required of me even though I cannot comprehend why God allowed Jenni to die.

What I Needed to Remember

In order to love God in the darkness, I had to reflect on many truths I had already known about God and God's world. I was born in a small town in the Sandhills of North Carolina. As such, I grew up playing in the woods and streams around my home. There I became a lover of creation. I am awed by the power of the created order, the reliability of scientific laws, the vast size of the universe, and the sheer beauty that is in every part of creation. The old hymn has it right: "this *is* my Father's world." To understand why bad events happen in the world, it is vital to understand the world as it was designed to be and the world as it is.

The Created Order

The first chapters of Genesis contain the narrative of the creation of the world. The story exists to teach us that the world was not the result of a great cosmic accident. Primordial geological forces and physical realities alone cannot explain the wonder of existence. There is existence because there is a Creator. The cosmos is the result of the work of God. Because God created it, we can expect the creation to point to God. The created order reflects the One who created it. In the words of the psalmist, "The heavens declare the glory of God" (Ps 19:1). In the Genesis narrative, the word used to describe the creation is "good." In the thirty-one verses of Genesis 1, the word "good" is used seven times. A basic rule of biblical interpretation I like to follow is this: if the Bible repeats something, it is important. When a word is used seven times in thirty-one verses, the author is practically shouting to the reader. Genesis wants you to know that God's creation is *very* good.

The Great Smokies

When seeing creation at its most beautiful, "good" seems almost too feeble a word to describe it. Running along the North Carolina-Tennessee border, the Great Smoky Mountains earn their name from the fog that often covers the peaks. The Cherokees originally named the mountains *Shaconage*, meaning "place of blue smoke."[8] The "smoke" that covers the mountains is a biological wonder. The dense forests covering the mountains emit particles called "terpenes" that interact with the ozone in the atmosphere. When moisture condenses on these particles, it scatters the blue and violet spectrums of light, causing the "smoke."[9] If you have ever seen the Great Smokies in their glory, you know. They are absolutely beautiful. They are stunning.

During the fall of the year, the Great Smokies put on a more colorful show. Usually in October, leaves on the trees in the upper elevations begin to change color, and the lower elevations follow later. The change of colors in the fall is truly striking. Driving through the Great Smokies during the fall is almost an act of worship.

I had the privilege of living in the North Carolina mountains for four years during my college experience at Western Carolina University (WCU). I still remember the exact moment I decided to attend Western. My mother and I went on a campus tour at WCU. It was a long drive from Rockingham to Cullowhee, about five hours. As we got near Cullowhee, we rounded one of the many bends in the road, and there in the distance below was WCU. It was a beautiful sight in the late spring, and I knew instantly that I was home. Even though my college experience was many years ago, and even though it was only a short span of my life, part of me will always belong in the mountains. Spending four years with mountains outside of your window instills in you a great respect for the beauty of creation.

If one looks at the grandeur of the Great Smokies and the rest of the North Carolina mountains, one can see the goodness of God's creation. The Great Smokies are very, very good.

The Human Brain

The instrument that makes observing creation possible, the human brain, is a masterpiece of design and function. Scientists are now only beginning to understand how the brain works. Weighing in at 3 pounds, a healthy human brain contains 200 billion nerve cells.[10] The cells are connected to each other by *trillions* of synapses. In the cerebral cortex alone, there are roughly 125 trillion synapses, about the number of stars it would take to fill 1,500 Milky Way Galaxies.[11]

The human brain regulates automatic functioning, controls the senses, stores our memories, interprets the information it receives from the nerves in the rest of the body, enables thought, empowers emotions, creates consciousness, and serves as the seat of the soul. Every thought you have ever had, every feeling you have ever felt, every movement you have ever undertaken, every sensory experience you have ever had originated in your brain.

Most of the brain's operation is automatic and we are unaware of it. It regulates our heartbeat, breathing, walking, sleep cycles, hearing, sight, and many other functions without us even having to think about it. That much is beyond debate. There is, however, a debate among brain scientists about the conscious part of our brain. Some argue that our conscious mind is the last to know about things. Neuroscientist David Eagleman puts it this way: "There is debate in the field about where consciousness even has efficacy. . . . By the time your conscious mind registers something, is it always just the last guy to get the news, and it doesn't even matter what it thinks?"[12] Eagleman argues that our conscious minds are really just a summary of what the rest of the brain is up to all the time, without us having any idea.[13]

While the jury is out on Eagleman's theories, one fact remains: the human brain is a masterpiece of complexity and design. While often compared to a computer, the human brain's connection and complexity far outpace computers. In fact, a single human brain has more switches than all the computers, routers, and internet connections on earth.[14] To put it directly, "The human brain is the most complex structure in the universe."[15]

As much as scientists have discovered about the brain, one great mystery remains. We cannot explain how the brain produces consciousness.[16] Naturalistic theories simply cannot account for consciousness at this point. While that may change sometime in the future, suffice it to say that our minds and how consciousness is produced in us is a profound mystery. The human brain, then, is a magnificent structure whose mysteries still elude solving.

If one looks at the power, complexity, and mysteries of the human brain, one has to agree with Genesis: it is very, very good.

Even the Loathsome

It is easy to see the goodness of the created order when one considers many majestic creatures. When one hears the lion roar or sees the eagle dive toward its prey, God's majesty can be readily seen. God's goodness, however, can be seen even in creatures we might find loathsome.

It was a rather ordinary late summer day. I was coming home from work, and I parked my car at the left door of our two-car garage. Walking toward the control panel to open the door, I noticed something move. Coiled at the corner of the right garage door, something slithered. It was a copper-head. The mere sight of him shot a shiver up my spine. I wanted to find a shovel to dispose of the snake immediately. So I punched in the code to open the garage door and find my weapon. Suddenly, the snake slithered under the garage door on the other side. When the door opened in front of me, I could not find him anywhere. There is only one thing worse than seeing a snake enter your garage—and that is not being able to *find* the snake in your garage. I walked gingerly around the garage, looking for the slithery intruder. Eventually, I threw snake repellent all over the garage, hoping he would expose himself or leave. I never found him.

Humans and snakes have a complicated relationship that I suspect dates to the garden of Eden. Personally, I hate them. I especially hate venomous vipers like copperheads. They are dangerous, and their bites can cause harm—even death. When I think about copperheads at a safe distance, however, they too show the creative power of God. In fact, their coloring is amazing. The pattern on their backs and the distinctive color on their heads is quite beautiful. Beauty can also be observed on the Brazilian boa, the Eastern diamond-back rattlesnake, the coral snake, and many other species of snakes as well. Yes, even the loathsome snake is a beautiful thing.

Copperheads are also masterful hunters. They, like other pit vipers, have areas between their eyes and nostrils that can sense heat. Using this capacity to track their targets, they are excellent hunters of the small creatures they see as prey. When attacking a larger target, they strike and wait for their poison to work so they can then attack a weakened enemy. While I might think of them as horrible creatures, God has invested in them beauty and wisdom. They are masterfully designed to live on the earth God has created, even while being detested by humans.

From the stunning to the intricate, from the majestic to the loathsome, the created order is a magnificently designed, brilliantly implemented act of God's power and wonder. There is beauty to behold in animals, mountains, oceans, and plants. From great evergreen trees to garden weeds, God has bathed our world with beauty, power, and majesty.

Something Is Wrong

One could be tempted to leave it there: the universe is very, very good. Leaving it there, however, would mean ignoring another part of human life. There is something terribly wrong with creation. The same cosmos that hosts the Great Smoky Mountains, the human brain, and the majestic beauty of creation also hosts events that cause massive suffering.

On December 26, 2004, at 7:59 a.m., a 9.3-magnitude earthquake struck in the Indian Ocean. The earthquake moved 750 miles of underwater earth at the fault line up to 40 feet. It lasted for ten minutes. The energy released in the earthquake is estimated to be more than two times greater than *all* of the bombs used during World War II. The moving of earth caused a massive displacement of water leading directly to a tsunami.[17]

The city of Banda Aceh in the north of Sumatra, an island in Western Indonesia, was closest to the epicenter of the earthquake. Within minutes, a 100-foot wall of water struck the city, killing more than 100,000 people. "Buildings folded like houses of cards, trees and cars were swept up in the oil-black rapids and virtually no one caught up in the deluge survived."[18] The death toll in Indonesia was estimated to be between 130,000 and 160,000 people. About a third of the victims were children. In total, 190,000 people were confirmed to have perished with over 40,000 missing and presumed dead.[19]

In great tragedies like this, a large number of fatalities can numb the mind. So it is helpful to look at the suffering on a smaller scale. In a haunting story, Eastern Orthodox theologian David Bentley Hart writes,

> there appeared a report from Sri Lanka recounting, in part, the story of a large man of enormous physical strength who was unable to prevent four of his five children from perishing in the tsunami, and who—as he recited the names of his lost children to the reporter, in descending order of age, ending with the name of his four-year-old-son—was utterly overwhelmed by his own weeping.[20]

Earthquakes have frequently had tragic consequences. The unnamed man from Sri Lanka is not alone in losing children to earthquakes and resulting tsunamis. An earthquake that historians, philosophers, and theologians frequently reference occurred November 1, 1755, in Lisbon, Portugal. Because the earthquake occurred during the hour of worship on All Saints Day, many of the residents of Lisbon were at worship in one of the numerous cathedrals in the city. Within minutes of the start of the tremors, many buildings, cathedrals included, began to collapse. Many who died were crushed under the ruins of their cathedrals. Shortly after the earthquake, a fire began. The city burned for five days. Approximately two-thirds of the city was destroyed by the earthquake and the fire.[21] Many citizens sought safety by the shoreline in the immediate aftermath of the earthquake. Tragically, many of them were lost in the tsunami the earthquake generated. Estimated fatalities were between 60,000 to 100,000 people.

Unfortunately, earthquakes are a normal part of planet Earth. William Broad writes, "The type of geological process that causes earthquakes and tsunamis is an essential characteristic of Earth. As far as scientists know, it does not occur on any other planetary body and has something very directly to do with the fact the Earth is a habitable planet."[22]

So what should we make of the world? It is beautiful and wonderful. It is also capable of causing massive destruction. Not only are there earthquakes; there are tornadoes and lightning. There are hurricanes and floods. These natural events are normal, and they even seem to be needed for planet Earth to sustain life.

Recent theologians seem to be torn over the nature of the created order. Some, following John Calvin, argue that every event is the result of the divine decree. If an earthquake happens, it is because God *has caused it to happen.* Calvin himself would not make a distinction between what God causes and what God allows.[23] No, every event is born of God's governance. While we may not be able to make sense of that governance, God is at work in every event. Our limited perspective may not see how an earthquake reflects the will of God, but we are to be assured that it is God's plan. The earthquake, these people say, may be for punishment of the wicked, to remind God's people to repent, or to cause God's people to depend wholly on God. In truth, we may never know the purposes of God, but we are to trust that God is good and right in everything God does.

Others have concluded that God has created a world governed by natural laws. Because God values an orderly creation, God rarely intervenes in earthly events. God's goodness in the created order dictates that the created order has a positive side and a negative side. The creation has light and darkness, warm and cold, life and death. These things are not evidence of a defective creation but of the wonder of it. Creation is perfect the way it is, disasters included.

What I have concluded is that the world is full of all the goodness that we observe, but it is also a *fallen* world. The Bible does not say how exactly, but something has gone terribly wrong in creation. In the Genesis narrative of the fall, God curses the ground, frustrating the work humans would need to do for survival. In the book of Romans, Paul argues that the creation itself groans under duress, waiting for its liberation from the bondage of sin and death. Looking at the whole narrative of the Bible, the story begins in paradise and ends in paradise. What happens in between is located in a broken universe distant from God.

In other words, the world we experience is not the world of creation. Because the world is broken, it can create both rainbows and volcanoes. Brokenness is the reason the same world that seems solid and safe is also dependent on earthquakes to make life possible. The same body that hosts the human brain can also host cancer. Events of "natural evil"[24] cruelly testify to the broken, fallen nature of our world.

Knowledge of the Fallen World Helps Us Heal

This revelation helped my healing significantly. Rather than blaming God for "taking" my sister, I could find hope in God's goodness. I came to believe that Jenni's cancer did not come into her life because God wanted it there. God is the author of life, not death. God consistently brought good into Jenni's life and into mine. Jenni's short life was filled with wonderful friends, a fine husband, a loving family, and the grace of God. God no more willed her to die than God willed evil in the first place.

To be fair, I believe God had the power to heal Jenni and did not. This side of eternity, I will never understand why, and sometimes I am okay with that. One facet of the healing process we have to get accustomed to is that healing does not often happen quickly. Grief travels its own course, and its timing is its own. It took me a very long time to let go of my anger, and it was something I could not consciously do. It happened little by little, and just as with the healing of an old physical injury, I hardly noticed it happening.

This is not to say that I have fully healed. I am pretty sure I have not. If healing means that I hurt no longer, I am sure I will not heal. I asked Josh how he healed, and I think his answer is instructive. He said, "In some ways, I don't know that you ever heal. There is a part of you that feels, incomplete, scarred, like an ending that has been taken away." While Josh is right, it is not the whole story. With time and God's grace, one becomes open to life again. One can let go of bitterness and anger. One can begin to embrace new adventures and begin to live again.

My first steps toward healing and Josh's first steps toward healing were almost mirror images of each other. For Josh, a change at work was required. At the time of Jenni's passing, she and Josh were both teachers. They taught the same subject; Jenni just taught the next grade level up. Nightly, they would make lesson plans and grade papers side by side. After losing Jenni, Josh could not continue to teach. Every day at work was a reminder of her passing. Every night featured an empty chair where she should sit. Every new lesson plan was a reminder that she was gone. On many occasions, Jenni had told Josh that she believed he would be an excellent counselor. Realizing his need for a change, Josh started a master's degree program in counseling. His first class was on grief. He wanted to learn how to emotionally process what had happened. He wanted to learn how to counsel himself. What he learned in the process was that God had given him the opportunity to help others who had similar experiences.

For me, it was the opposite process. While Josh needed to emotionally process what had happened, I needed to intellectually process what had happened even as my world collapsed. I decided to enter a PhD program in systematic theology and study the problem of evil. From 2012 to 2018, I studied the problem of evil in order to come to some understanding of the ways of God and the presence of evil. My study has allowed me to enter conversation with those whose faith in God has been shaken by their experiences.

While I do not have a complete answer to the problem of evil, it is enough for me to know that Jenni left this earth to be in the presence of the One who has loved her from eternity past and will love her forever. Jenni may not be in my presence anymore, but she will forever be in God's presence. By God's grace, I will be with her and with God in a day yet to come.

We also have to accept that while this may be our Father's world, it is our Father's *broken* world. God, in goodness and grace, will heal this world and us on God's time schedule. Neither of those may be when we would want, but through faith we will see it when it happens. So we pray with the earliest believers, "Come quickly, Lord Jesus."

CHAPTER 5

Telling the Truth to God

One of the dearest people in my spiritual journey is Janet King. Janet has always been a hero of mine. I actually shudder to call her "Janet" because for most of my life I have known her as Mrs. King. She was my English, Spanish, and civics teacher my senior year in high school, and my mother taught me to use formal names for people who have earned respect. Only when I reached adulthood did Janet absolve me of that responsibility, and I begrudgingly agreed. Janet is obviously a very intelligent and talented woman, but what impresses me the most about her is her joyful spiritual nature. The Lord brings joy to her life every day. That much is obvious any time you speak with her. I look up to her for that, and I find in her life a model of the kind of spiritual life I am trying to cultivate.

After I lost Jenni, and after my marriage was done, I reached out to Janet. We had lost touch over many years, but I wanted—needed—to talk to someone. I needed a friend. So I found her phone number. We talked about our lives, we talked about Jenni, and we talked about her son.

Janet's son Michael was about two years older than me. Mike, as I knew him, was extremely bright and had great potential. Mike and I attended Temple Christian School together for a couple of years, but he transferred to the large public school in our county for the last few years of his high school experience. I lost touch with Michael during my college years. I knew he had gone into the Navy, but that was about it. As Janet informed me, Mike had later enlisted in the Army and had planned to be a veterinarian. During the Second Gulf War, Michael was stationed in Iraq. On August 10, 2007, Michael was killed. Janet responded the way any mother would to this news: she was devastated.

In describing the ordeal of his loss Janet wrote,

> So, when I heard Michael had died, I was able to say, "The Lord gives and the Lord takes away. Blessed be the name of the Lord," but later it was not so easy. Reality set in, and there were nights—grief is always harder at night—when I found myself unable to connect with the truth I have believed and lived and taught for many years. That disconnect culminated in one very dark night when I looked up at the ceiling, shook my fist and said, "If this is love, then I'll pass; don't tell me you understand, because You got Your son back, and I won't. Leave me alone. . . . I hate you."

These were raw words. They were, however, true. Janet was crushed. Her son was gone, and that was not going to change. While she is not proud of the words she spoke to and about God, they might have been the most important first step toward healing.

The process of healing from spiritual and emotional trauma often begins with telling the truth. Of course, we cannot tell the truth until we can face the truth. Facing the truth, however, is not easily done. It is much easier to live with our well-worn comfortable clichés about how the world works. We like to believe that we can find a reason for everything, that good things happen to good people, and that the world has a rational, orderly structure that humans can discern. But the world is more complicated than our clichés.

Truth is much harder. It requires dealing with the reality we face and not the world as we wish it were. While facing the truth is difficult and unpleasant, hiding from the truth actively prevents our healing. We must tell the whole unvarnished truth to God, even if—maybe especially if—we are angry.

Some may recoil against expressing anger toward God. It sounds, well, blasphemous. Consider who God is. God is holy and omnipotent. God's goodness knows no bounds. God is beyond us. We have no capacity to judge God's actions. We have no right to second-guess God's providence. God will not surrender God's majesty to humans, who have not the perspective or righteousness to judge God.

The Scriptures, however, teach us that God *already* knows everything, even our anger against God. Psalm 44:21 teaches us that God already knows the secrets of our hearts. In an amazing testament to God's knowledge, Psalm 139:1-12 reads,

> O LORD, you have searched me and known me.
> You know when I sit down and when I rise up;
> You discern my thoughts from far away.
> You search out my path and my lying down,
> And are acquainted with all my ways.
> Even before a word is on my tongue,
> O Lord, you know it completely
> You hem me in, behind and before,
> And lay your hand upon me.

Such knowledge is too wonderful for me;
It is so high that I cannot attain it.
Where can I go from your spirit?
Or where can I flee from your presence?
If I ascend to heaven, you are there;
If I make my bed in Sheol, you are there.
If I take the wings of the morning and settle at the
    farthest limits of the sea,
Even there your hand shall lead me,
And your right hand shall hold me fast.
If I say, "Surely the darkness shall cover me, and the light
    around me become night,"
Even the darkness is not dark to you;
the night is as bright as the day,
for darkness is as light to you.

In this psalm, David points us to the crucial truth: there is no place where we can hide from God. There is no place in all of creation where God cannot see. There is no word we can speak that God does not know. Our habits and foibles are known to God already. Even if we were among the dead, God could see us there. Even the dark is not a place to hide from God. We have no thought that God does not already know. Failure to express our thoughts about God to God does not protect God's majesty. It only prevents our healing.

It is interesting that we can note the power of God's knowledge and yet not express our anger to God. Perhaps we think it is sinful to express certain thoughts to God. I suppose it could be sinful to lash out at God, but on the other hand, would it also not be destructive to our relationship with God to fail to tell God the truth? Is it not also sinful to cover up our feelings with religious-sounding platitudes?

What if expressing anger at God is not blasphemous at all? What if there were evidence that expressing honest, raw emotion was a real part of the spiritual journey? There are texts in the Bible where people reflect candid emotions to God.

In a section that is often called the Minor Prophets, in the book of Habakkuk, the prophet complains directly to God about God's inaction.

> How long, O LORD, will I call for help, and you will not hear? I cry out to you, "Violence!" Yet you do not save. Why do you make me see iniquity, and cause me to look on wickedness? Yes, destruction and violence are before me; strife exists and contention arises. Therefore, the law is ignored and justice is never upheld. For the wicked surround the righteous; therefore, justice comes out perverted. (Hab 1:2-4 NRSV)

Habakkuk reflects a common human emotion. He is exasperated at God's inaction. His world is full of violence, and God seems to do nothing. God seems to tolerate evil and oppression. The law, God's gift to the Hebrew people, has proven to be ineffective against those who would ignore it. We can feel the defeat in Habakkuk's words: "justice *never* emerges."

If it is acceptable for Habakkuk to express such a defeated spirit, how can it not be acceptable for us? If Habakkuk can say that God does nothing in the face of violence, it must be acceptable for us to do the same.

I did not want to tell God about my anger. I *wanted* to be angry at God. I was determined to hold God's inaction against God until the end. I felt that talking to God about my anger and even receiving healing was a betrayal of Jenni. I did not want to forgive God. I know how ludicrous that sounds. God is God. I am not. I have no grounds to judge God. I have no basis for asserting that somehow I know better than God what God ought to do. I am a sinner with no standing before God other than God's grace. The mere idea of a human having a case against God is laughable and an insult to reason. When a heart is shattered, though, reason does not work properly. In the end, I would have been much better off to follow Janet's path of just telling the truth to God.

One should, however, be prepared when expressing such raw emotion to God. God's response to Habakkuk is to totally change his perspective on the problem of evil. God shows Habakkuk that his observations of God's inactivity are mistaken. God states that God's work will leave Habakkuk utterly stunned. It will leave him so shocked that he would not have believed it even if he had been told. God is working, and Habakkuk's charge of inaction has no merit.

God is more than capable of challenging your perspective; in fact, you should expect it. God is still God, after all. Telling the truth may result in God revealing a truth to you that leaves you breathless. Do not be afraid, though. God is working for good and healing.

Telling the Truth

I am a quiet man. I do not often speak of my emotions. In truth, I do not handle them as well as I wish. I tend to keep the deep reservoirs of my feelings pent up inside, and often no one really knows what is going on in my heart. I only opened up about the aftermath of Jenni's loss years after the fact when I wrote a handful of blog posts that documented my struggles. In the days that followed, I received a few phone calls. The first was from a lifelong friend. He called to apologize. He said he wished he could have been there for me and was sorry that he was not. His absence was not his fault. How could he have known that my life was descending into darkness? I never told him. The second call was from my father. He called to make sure I was okay. He said he had never known that this period of time in my life was so difficult. I never told him either. I am pretty sure I never told anyone how dark a place I was in.

You may suspect that my not opening up is due to some sort of John Wayne masculinity—that I was just trying to be tough through an ordeal. Perhaps that was part of the issue, but the bottom line is that I have never made a practice of letting people know what is going on inside of me. Some have said I'm like Fort Knox. I suppose that is true. In all candor, my reticence has often served me well. Holding back intimate details of what is going on is a good way to protect one's heart from betrayal. Unfortunately, it also prevents one from reaching out to those who could help during times of crisis.

None of this is the way God intended it. Friends are a gift of God. They are great during the high points of life. Friends enrich our lives as we gather to watch a game, share a laugh, or enjoy company together. According to the Mayo Clinic, having close friends is good for our health.[25] Friends can improve our sense of purpose, improve our self-image, help us avoid toxic habits, and reduce our stress. Friends help reduce the risk of major diseases and even obesity.[26] Little wonder then why they are so important to us. They make our lives better. Friends are there for us when we are in the darkness. It would have been much better for me to have reached out to my friends. I know they would have been there for me had I allowed them. David had Jonathan. Jesus had Peter, James, and John. If you have people in your life who love you, you never have to be alone. You never have to suffer in silence. I have a few close friends. The problem is that I never brought them into my story.

Family, like friendship, is a gift from God. While much is written in psychological literature about the role of family dysfunction in our various psychological traumas, family itself is vital for our health. Without a healthy family background, we are more likely to have mental illness and even a greater penchant for lawlessness behavior.

Family also gives us a reservoir of outside wisdom. Near the beginning of Israel's sojourn in the wilderness, Moses' father-in-law, Jethro, came for a visit. Jethro wanted to visit with his daughter and grandchildren. He listened to the remarkable story Moses told about the liberation of the people from slavery in Egypt. Jethro worshiped God with Moses and shared a meal in the presence of God. Then Jethro watched. Jethro watched as Moses sat down to judge the people from the morning till the evening. Jethro saw and knew that what Moses was doing was not good. Moses was going to work himself to death trying to settle disputes between people. Moses as the sole judge for the people was not only inefficient; it was destructive. Jethro suggested that Moses appoint leaders over groups of people and only decide the difficult matters himself.

In Moses' case, family made an enormous positive difference in the way he led Israel. Family can make an important contribution to our spiritual good as well. Family is a treasure to lean on, and a healthy family can help us withstand just about any crisis.

I had family who cared, but I did not reach out to them. Part of the reason I was reluctant to talk to my family was due to the nature of the multiple crises affecting me. What was going on at home was private. Inviting my family in would have made family gatherings awkward. What was going on medically was private as well; I was concerned they would badger me with quick-fix treatments. The spiritual darkness surrounding me was something I did not have the words to express. So I did not try to express it, even to my family.

I was also silent with my church. When one preaches, one bears one's soul. This is even true when one tries not to be self-referential. How you are comes through in preaching. So my congregation intuitively knew something was up. They did not know what or even what it meant. They did know, however, that something was not right with me. It takes a brave pastor to open up to members of his congregation, even privately. I did not have that kind of courage. As much as God has given us friends and family, God has given us the body of Christ. They are there for us. When you are in a crisis, they will pray with you and for you. They will honor your journey. Yes, some will try to solve your problems. Others will not recognize how bad your situation is. On the other hand, a true, faithful, believing congregation will make your life much better. I thought I was being strong by carrying my burdens all alone. I felt that it was right and good to bear my suffering without involving my church. In truth, I was falling apart quickly, and I was being foolish.

I know now, and should have known then, that there were people in my congregation who would have listened to me share my struggles and would have cared about me. At the time, I only knew of the isolation of ministry. I did not share because it felt unsafe to share. Because I shut out my friends, my family, and my church, I was missing three levels of support God has designed for believers to have.

In November 2013, I experienced the power of the church to care and learned how much easier it would have been to invite them into my struggle. Thanksgiving came, and my family of origin had its celebration the weekend before the holiday. That year, it was not my holiday to have my daughter with me, so I expected to spend Thanksgiving Day alone. I nearly despaired at the thought, and I frantically tried to make plans. Two church families realized what was happening and took me into their homes. One invited me over for lunch. Another invited me over for dinner. I was not alone because they cared about me immensely. Thanksgiving was not the horrible day I feared after all. My life was better because they wanted me to be with them.

Telling the truth to God, my friends, my family, and my church would have made my life so much better. It would have started the healing process sooner.

Recovery

My friend Janet talks of her recovery. After that night when she shook her fist at heaven over the death of her son, she woke early in the morning as always. She made her coffee and wanted more than anything to do her normal prayer and Bible reading. God met her there that morning, knowing what had occurred the night before.

Regarding her angry outburst at God, she reflects,

> I'm not proud of that behavior at all, but the way God loved me and held me even in that outburst is hard to explain. Truth went from my head to my heart in a new way. We really do not have to hide our emotions from our Father. . . . After my outburst I fell asleep and slept the best sleep I had since Michael's passing. When I woke up the next morning, all I could think of was getting to my Bible and meeting with the Lord. I felt as if He said to me, "I will never let you go, even when you *think* you want me to."

CHAPTER 6

The Psalms Are Your Friend

Some time ago, I read that Billy Graham started his day by reading five psalms and one chapter of Proverbs. I reasoned that if it were good enough for Billy Graham, it would be good enough for me. Ever since, the book of Psalms has been a staple of my spiritual journey. The psalms are unique in the way they come to us. Most of the Bible comes as God's speech to humans. "Thus says the LORD," we read. Many of the psalms, on the contrary, are human speech to God.[27] Some of them express simple trust and joy. Others express outrage at a world gone mad. Others express something akin to hatred for those who have inflicted horrors on the people of Israel. Still others express deep frustration, even anger, toward God. Taken as a whole, they are a treasure of the life of faith.

Biblical scholar Walter Brueggemann likes to think of three different kinds of psalms. He calls them psalms of orientation, psalms of disorientation, and psalms of new orientation.[28] While I would not necessarily use his language, he is on to something important. The psalms express faithful devotion to God when things are good, when things are broken, and when things are made right again.

When All Is Well

Brueggemann's psalms of orientation are psalms for when everything is right with our world. He writes, "Human life consists in satisfied seasons of well-being that evoke gratitude for the constancy of blessing."[29] When our lives are settled, when our children are happy and healthy, when our occupations are successful, when our marriages are good, we want to express ourselves in joyful tones, confident in the world and trusting in the One who has made the world to be so good. For example, look at Psalm 19:

> The heavens declare the glory of God; the skies proclaim the work of his hands.
> Day after day they pour forth speech; night after night they reveal knowledge.
> They have no speech, they use no words; no sound is heard from them.
> Yet their voice goes out into all the earth, their words to the ends of the world.
> In the heavens God has pitched a tent for the sun.
> It is like a bridegroom coming out of his chamber,
> Like a champion rejoicing to run his course.
> It rises at one end of the heavens and makes its circuit to the other;
> Nothing is deprived of its warmth.
> The law of the LORD is perfect, refreshing the soul.
> The statutes of the LORD are trustworthy, making wise the simple.
> The precepts of the LORD are right, giving joy to the heart.
> The commands of the LORD are radiant, giving light to the eyes.

The fear of the LORD is pure, enduring forever.
The decrees of the LORD are firm, and all of them are
    righteous.
They are more precious than gold, than much pure gold;
They are sweeter than honey, than honey from the
    honeycomb.
By them your servant is warned; in keeping them there
    is great reward.
But who can discern their own errors?
Forgive my hidden faults.
Keep your servant also from willful sins; may they not
    rule over me.
Then I will be blameless, innocent of great transgression.
May these words of my mouth and this meditation of
    my heart be pleasing in your sight,
LORD, my Rock and my Redeemer. (NIV)

C. S. Lewis said about Psalm 19, "I take this to be the greatest poem in the Psalter and one of the greatest lyrics in the world."[30] The psalm is rightly marveled at for its beauty of expression and love for the Creator. Its argument is plain: the wonder of the creation expresses the majesty of the Creator.

Even though creation is wordless, the psalmist argues, it expresses the wonder of the Creator to everyone who is willing to look. In Christmastime of 2020, many looked to the sky to see what some astronomers called the "Christmas Star." What they were viewing was the conjunction of Saturn and Jupiter. A conjunction happens when two objects in space appear to come together when viewed from earth. In actuality, these celestial objects are millions of miles apart. When viewed from earth, though, a conjunction appears to give off a much brighter light than either of the other two objects would individually. The Saturn-Jupiter conjunction was the first time the conjunction between the two planets was visible from earth in 800 years. After getting a glimpse of it in the night sky, I have to say it was very bright and impressive. A long gaze at the conjunction could easily yield the kind of praise Psalm 19 expresses.

And so much more points to the glory of God. The brightness of the moon on a dark night, the pale green and red colors of the northern lights, the passing of a comet, the North Star—all of these combine as if they were one giant choir singing the praises of the One who made them. Some time ago, I was speaking with an atheist who could not believe God would create all of space just for us. I replied, "God did not create it for us. He created it for Him." The universe is created out of the bliss of God. It belongs to God, and no doubt God enjoys God's handiwork. It is *very good.*

Psalm 19 not only expresses wonder at creation; it expresses gratitude for the Law. The author views the Mosaic Law as a gift. Contrary to many modern Christians who have come to see it as an undue burden, the psalmist expresses a belief that a right understanding of the Law is essential for a good life. Far from being a burden, the Law is perfect. It is trustworthy. It is radiant and enlightens life. It is pure and firm. It provides a trustworthy foundation. Keeping the Law results in a great reward.

At the end of the psalm, the writer expresses not only his love for God but also a spirit of humility. "May these words of my mouth and this meditation of my heart be acceptable in your sight . . . ." It is as if he wants to make sure the psalm itself expresses his worship for God in a way that God finds honoring. It is as if he is saying, "The God who created all of existence is beyond imagination, and I hope these words— the best expressions I have—are up to the task of honoring God."

When All Is Lost

What kind of person might create a majestic writing like Psalm 19? The superscription says it is a Psalm of David. David, the second and greatest of Israel's kings, was regarded as a "man after God's own heart." In his younger years, David defeated a giant, avoided his predecessor's—King Saul's—irrational wrath, became an expert at music and writing, became a brilliant military strategist, and eventually became king. David's story is not all good, however. There are some dark chapters in David's story.

Satisfied with the success of his reign and confident in his military advisors, David remained home from battle in his siege against Rabbah. His decision was a violation of the purity laws of warfare, and it set David up for a disaster. From his rooftop porch David gazed down at Jerusalem below him and saw a strikingly beautiful woman, Bathsheba. Inquiring who she was, David discovered her name and learned that she was the wife of Uriah, most likely a member of David's elite guard. David sent messengers to get her and brought her to his palace. He slept with her and she conceived. Modern scholars are quick to call this event something akin to rape. The text, however, does not say that. It can only be noted that from Bathsheba's perspective, saying "no" to the king would have been *very* difficult. Whether it was rape or consensual, David now had a problem. Bathsheba was carrying his child, and Uriah had been on the battlefield too long to be the child's father. David tried to get Uriah to violate his oath of purity and sleep with Bathsheba to make the child plausibly Uriah's. Uriah, however, having more honor than David, would not. David then resorted to a sinister plot and had Uriah killed in battle. At a minimum, David committed adultery and murder. (See 2 Samuel 11.)

As a result, God punished David. Pointedly, the prophet Nathan told David the sword would never depart from his house. One such instance occurs in 2 Samuel 15. In this text, David is pictured as a pathetic figure. One of David's sons, Absalom, had regularly undermined the David's rule, and his strategy was effective. Absalom, who was a handsome and charismatic figure, developed an entourage of fifty men who would go before him and shout his praises. He would enter Jerusalem, stand at the gate, and insinuate to those who had grievances that King David would not provide justice for them. He would suggest that if only he were in charge, their cries would be heard. His persistent insinuations, charm, and good looks eventually paid off. Absalom "stole the hearts of the men of Israel" (15:6). The people preferred Absalom to David. Even as David held the throne, Absalom was already the preferred king in the people's hearts. Revolution was brewing, and Absalom was at the center of it.

Because the people were with Absalom and Absalom planned to seize the throne, David had to flee Jerusalem. Second Samuel 15 presents David walking up the Mount of Olives with his head covered, shoeless, and weeping as he flees Absalom's vile assault. David's appearance indicated mourning. He could hardly have looked less inspirational. He was no longer the courageous young man facing down Goliath. He was not rallying soldiers to put down raiders as he did when he avoided Saul's fury. No, here David looked every bit like a broken man. Could the David of 2 Samuel 15 have composed Psalm 19? I think not, at least not at that moment.

We are not always the kind of people who feel like David did when he wrote Psalm 19. The human experience, the faith experience, is much more varied than that. I'm grateful that there are other psalms. I'm grateful that the David of

2 Samuel 15 does not have to pretend to be something other than he is.

What kind of psalm might a person write if facing something like David did in 2 Samuel 15? Consider these words from Psalm 69, also "of David":

Save me, O God,
For the waters have threatened my life.
I have sunk in deep mire, and there is no foothold;
I have come into deep waters, and a flood overflows me.
I am weary with my crying; my throat is parched;
My eyes fail while I wait for my God.
Those who hate me without a cause are more than the
    hairs of my head;
Those who would destroy me are powerful, being wrong-
    fully my enemies;
What I did not steal, I then have to restore.
O God, it is You who knows my folly,
And my wrongs are not hidden from You.
May those who wait for You not be ashamed through
    me, O Lord GOD of hosts;
May those who seek You not be dishonored through me,
    O God of Israel,
Because for Your sake I have borne reproach;
Dishonor has covered my face.
I have become estranged from my brothers
And an alien to my mother's sons.
For zeal for Your house has consumed me,
And the reproaches of those who reproach You have
    fallen on me.
When I wept in my soul with fasting,
It became my reproach.
When I made sackcloth my clothing,
I became a byword to them.
Those who sit in the gate talk about me,
And I am the song of the drunkards.

But as for me, my prayer is to You, O LORD, at an
    acceptable time;
O God, in the greatness of Your lovingkindness,
Answer me with Your saving truth.
Deliver me from the mire and do not let me sink;
May I be delivered from my foes and from the deep
    waters.
May the flood of water not overflow me
Nor the deep swallow me up,
Nor the pit shut its mouth on me.
Answer me, O LORD, for Your lovingkindness is good;
According to the greatness of Your compassion, turn to
    me,
And do not hide Your face from Your servant,
For I am in distress; answer me quickly. (NASB 1995)

"I feel like I'm drowning," we might say. I rather suspect
that is the kind of thing a man who is fleeing for his life
might say. David had cried until his throat was parched. He
had been hated without cause. Now he was waiting. He was
waiting for God to deliver him, and even the waiting was
torment. He turned to God in prayer and he was mocked.
He fasted and he was rebuked. Silly drunks sang songs to
mock his plight. When he repented, he was insulted. What
he could not find was God.

Where was God? Why was the One who had so carefully
saved David on so many occasions suddenly become distant?
We do not know, and we do not know because *David* does
not know. Worse, no answer seems to be coming. David
admits it; he has sinned. If God is the God of mercy and
grace, why did David's repentance not quickly bring mercy?
As much as we would like to think so, mercy has not come.
David's eyes fail while he waits for God.

So how does David not give up? Why should the readers
of the psalm not give up? David finally does not give up

because he has confidence in God. He knows another day will come. Later in the psalm he writes,

> I will praise the name of God with song
> And magnify Him with thanksgiving.
> And it will please the LORD better than an ox
> Or a young bull with horns and hoofs. (NASB 1995)

David is confident in God because of *memory*. David has a long memory of God being at work in his life. God spared David from the paw of a lion, the paw of a bear, the strength of Goliath, and the rage of Saul. Because God had been faithful in the past, David knew God would be faithful in the future. While the duration of his sorrow was unknown, the end was sure.

David is also confident in God because of God's character. Verse 33 reads, "For the LORD hears the needy and does not despise those of His who are prisoners." God is, by definition, good. Because God is good, God cannot be less than good to God's people. There may be difficulty, and it may be prolonged. God, however, will never abandon God's people.

When life is dark, when I feel like I might drown, the most important thing for me to do is cling to God. Even when I cannot feel God's presence, God is there. Even when it seems like God is not listening, God is. Even when my world seems dark, God is light and there is no darkness in God at all, as 1 John 1:5 reminds us. I can love God in the darkness because I know who God is.

We also hold on to God in anticipation. When restoration comes, we will celebrate. We will celebrate the works of God with our most joyful expressions. God, ever in mercy, will receive it.

When Order Is Restored

Psalm 150 concludes the book of Psalms, serving as a final word. It is as if the Psalter is saying, "After all is concluded, after every deed is done, after every action is finished, the only thing left to do is to praise God." That kind of full-throated praise to God comes after the situation has changed. We have moved from simple trust and joy in God through a painful period where God seems to have vanished just when we need God most. Now, though, at the end, God is here and God is faithful.

A restored order does not mean everything is perfect. In my own journey of loss, order has been restored. I am not the broken man collapsed on the floor of my closet anymore. My spiritual life is whole. I no longer live in profound anger with God. Still, though, things are not as they were.

My faith is different now from what it was before. I bristle at easy appeals to optimism. I tend to focus on the eternal properties of faith rather than thinking of the temporal advantages of serving God. It is hard for me to think about God's providential care without thinking of the times when evil strikes. Although I know the number of times that God has provided for me and protected me and my family dwarfs the number of times that sorrow has struck, I still find it hard to let my full focus be on the good. I say that with great shame. I pray for God's help. I say this to note that the ending point is not the same as the starting point. There was a journey in between, a journey that cannot be erased.

Perhaps that is why in many of the psalms of deliverance the struggle prior to God's intervention is mentioned prominently.

I will extol You, O LORD, for You have lifted me up,
And have not let my enemies rejoice over me.
O LORD my God, I cried to You for help, and You
healed me.
O LORD, You have brought up my soul from Sheol;
You have kept me alive, that I would not go down to the
pit.
Sing praise to the LORD, you His godly ones,
And give thanks to His holy name.
For His anger is but for a moment, His favor is for a
lifetime;
Weeping may last for the night,
But a shout of joy comes in the morning.
Now as for me, I said in my prosperity, "I will never be
moved."
O LORD, by Your favor You have made my mountain to
stand strong;
You hid Your face, I was dismayed.
To You, O LORD, I called,
And to the Lord I made supplication:
"What profit is there in my blood, if I go down to the
pit?
Will the dust praise You? Will it declare Your faithful-
ness?
Hear, O LORD, and be gracious to me; O LORD, be my
helper."
You have turned for me my mourning into dancing;
You have loosed my sackcloth and girded me with glad-
ness,
That my soul may sing praise to You and not be silent.
O LORD my God, I will give thanks to You forever.
(Psalm 30:1-12)

David had been established; his "mountain," meaning the
power of God's kingdom, had been created and preserved by
God. God, however, hid God's face. The result was predictable: David entered a time of deep sorrow.

Sorrow, however, was not the end of the story. God turned sorrow into joy. Of course, that is always God's plan. The sorrow of loss is overwhelmed by the joy that awaits believers in the life to come. In Romans 8, Paul says the difficulties of this life are not worth comparing to the bliss of eternal life. Eternal life simply trivializes our present distress. For David, however, it was not the life to come that changed his mourning to dancing. It was God's action in David's circumstances. It is important to be careful and avoid any hint of prosperity theology. It is not proper to suggest that God's goal in our lives is temporal happiness and prosperity. God's goal for us is always Christlikeness. With that important caveat, know that God intervenes in our current circumstances to bring about joy and happiness more than we will ever know this side of eternity. God brings joy into our lives regularly and consistently. In fact, I believe that since joy is an outgrowth of goodness and God is the wellspring of all goodness, joy itself has its only source in God.

When the darkness is too much, it is enough to know that God will not forget God's people. God will turn your sorrow to joy and overwhelm your suffering with goodness.

The Psalms Have Comforting Power

Virtually every human emotion is expressed in the book of Psalms. The psalms contain gratitude for the nation and celebrations for the king. The psalms contain expressions of wonder at the goodness of God. They also contain discordant notes. There are rants directed to God about God's behavior. In the psalms are painful pleas asking where God is hiding. There are also psalms expressing unmitigated weeping in longing for God. Knowing that God has given us the psalms as a gift helps us recognize that in every facet of life there is a psalm that expresses our emotions. They are, then, a treasure of guidance and spiritual care given by God for our good.

Coming to Terms with God

The youth and children's director at my church was a particularly good friend during my darkest days. She would ask how I was doing and be genuinely interested in the answer. Most days, I did not want to go into much detail, and I did not want to lie. So I would summon my best *Life of Brian* impression and say, "I'm not dead!" Gallows humor, I suppose. In truth, I was "punch drunk." How I was still standing was beyond me, but I was standing. I suspect it was only by the grace of God.

I describe how I felt at the time as darkness. In the Bible and in early Christian thought, darkness is juxtaposed against light. God is light, and the absence of God is darkness. Grieving a lost sister, facing an inevitable divorce, and living in physical pain made me feel like God was nowhere to be found. It was very, very dark.

In the immediate wake of Jenni's loss, I thought the events would be a mortal blow to my faith. I imagined, like a character in a Tolkien novel, that I had received the fatal wound, but it would take several more tomes before the lethality of the wound was made manifest. Later, I came to think of myself like the biblical character of Jacob. I had the terrible wrestling match that lasted all night, and I would forever limp because of it. My first insight might have been closer to the truth than I would have imagined, however. There were parts of my faith that did die, and they needed to die.

The thing about God is that God is incomprehensible to us. If the philosophers and theologians I read are correct, we learn by analogy. We come to understand the object we see because it is like some other thing we know. The sidewalk is like the road; the eagle is like the hawk; my hands are like Mom's hands. God, however, is not an object of sense experience, so no comparison will work. God is utterly unique. As if that did not complicate things enough, God is utterly beyond us. God is infinite in God's being, unlimited in power, unyielding in opposition to evil, unaffected by time or space, and the ground of all existence. God is the ontological essence of good;[31] God is goodness itself.[32] God, having the fullness of all things available at all times to Godself, exists in pure eternal bliss. God is ever directed to the good of God's creation. In short, God is love.

Because everything that God is happens to be beyond human comprehension, we naturally try to find ways to explain God in human terms, if only to ourselves. Unfortunately for us, all of these attempts fail. Human attempts to define God end up describing a being that is like us, only bigger and more powerful. Barth would say these descriptions reduce God to "Man spoken in a loud voice." Our definitions of God are usually what we want or fear God to be. They are always idols of our own making. As John Calvin notes, the human heart is an idol factory.[33] What happens to us is that we become attached to these God definitions and think they *are* God. God, however, will not tolerate them.

My faith that suffered a mortal blow when Jenni died was not faith in God. It was faith in the God who did what I wanted God to do. It is like we humans have a little deal with God. We think that if we give our lives to Jesus, go to church, pray, and act like we have good sense, then God will bless us. God will grant us our hopes, keep us healthy, and help us pay the bills. God will keep our children safe and our siblings sane. God will make the bad people stay away and make the good ones learn to be decent company. When the little deal we have with God does not work out, we are bumfuzzled and often more than a little angry.

The problem is that God made no such deal with us. God never promised a life without suffering for God's children. It is only in recent times that humans have had the expectation that life should be without suffering. In fact, medieval Christian thinkers were afraid if they had too many blessings in their lives. They thought having too many blessings was evidence that they were getting rewarded on earth and that the afterlife would be terrible.[34] This idea that suffering should not exist is new. It is we—the people with running water and air conditioning, with the wisdom of the ages available on our smartphones, with seventy-inch UHDTVs adorning our walls, with forty-hour work weeks and paid vacations, with copious amounts of food and rivers of wine, with ever-increasing life spans and the ability to treat pain— who have decided that humans should never suffer and that a loving God would not allow them to.

The Bible never presents such a picture of life. Ezekiel suffered. Hosea suffered. Hannah suffered. Ruth suffered. John the Baptist suffered. Mary suffered. Paul suffered. Yes, Jesus suffered. For us to conclude that suffering will not be part of our lives is to ignore what the Bible teaches and to ignore reality.

God Is Good

Part of my faith that suffered a mortal wound was faith
in a particular kind of Divine Governance. While I found
the orderly, systematic nature of Calvinism attractive in
my college years, I eventually came to find it untenable.
In Calvinism, people do not come to faith on their own;
they do so because of the work of God. That is true in any
reading of the faith, but Calvinism takes it much further. For
John Calvin, it is not enough to say that no one comes to
God without God calling them. No, God calls only the ones
God chooses to call to salvation, and only to those whom
God wants to save will God give the ability to respond in
faith. Those who respond in faith are the ones God chose in
eternity past, and only them. Those who accept God's call
are the elect. Those who do not are the damned. What is the
difference between two groups? God's choice. So, if a person
goes to hell, it is because God chooses for them to go to hell.
This is called unconditional election. Election to eternal life
is unconditioned by the deeds or the future faith of those
whom God chooses.

In Calvin's view, God is the orchestrator of events. For
most believers, there is a difference between what God *causes*
and what God *allows*. Calvin rejects that out of hand. Everything happens because of God's choice for God's glory.

Here's an example. Go to your nearest children's hospital.
Why does the child in room 1 have AIDS? It was God's will,
and through that God will glorify Godself. Why does the
child in room 15 have cancer? It was God's will. Why did
the child in room 21 inherit a defective heart? Because of
God. Why is the child in the treatment room screaming for
Mom because of the needles and chemotherapy? Because

COMING TO TERMS WITH GOD

of God. For me, very personally, why is Jenni dead? I can't bring myself to say it.

If this is the way God works, what kind of God are we left with? According to Kate Bowler, "A woman who left the faith for science writes, 'I find it comforting to believe everything in the universe is random, because then the God I believe in is no longer cruel.'"[35] If we believe that God controls everything directly, if there is no distance between the Divine will and human suffering, then must we not think of God as cruel? If God causes suffering for the purpose of self-glorification, what else can we think of God?

I am not alone in rejecting Calvin's logic. But the company I keep gets smaller when it comes to how I view life on earth and God's governance. I now reject the idea that God orchestrates every event in my life. Just because something has happened is not evidence that God wanted it to happen. God may have allowed it, but the world is not micromanaged by God. If it were, we would have serious issues with God's character. For me, the Holocaust would rule out any easy connection between the world as it is and God's desires.

I believe the way to describe God's governance is to find a path between omnicausality and Deism. I'm using the term "omnicausality" to define a God who causes every single event by direct command—as in Calvinism. Deism is a philosophical view popular during the 1600s and 1700s arguing that God was the Master Creator who left the world to operate by its own natural laws.

For its many flaws, Deism noted that God had created a wonderful world operating by natural laws. The problem with Deism is that it is unwilling to suggest God's continual activity in the world. Deists correctly note that the world is orderly and magnificent. They don't accept, though, that

God actively maintains the world. God not only created the
atomic table but also sustains the universe by God's power.
Further, in direct contradiction to Deists, God intervenes in
the world at any time God likes.

For its many flaws, omnicausality notes that the world
is God's to do with as God chooses. God is the Lord of the
universe, and no one has the right to judge God. On the
other hand, what omnicausality omits is the radical goodness
of God. God has disclosed God's person as good, and the
Scriptures are full of that declaration. For the term "good" to
have any meaning, the Scriptures must be using it in a way
that is at least somewhat similar to what humans mean by
the use of the term. There is, of course, a radical distance. For
example, when the Bible teaches of the wisdom of Solomon,
his wisdom cannot even approximate the wisdom of God.
Solomon's wisdom and God's wisdom are infinitely different.[36] On the other hand, they are at least the same kind
of quality. So if the Bible says God is good, God's goodness
is infinitely better than the best of human goodness, but
it is goodness nonetheless. Must it not be the case that for
God to be good, God's goodness must be comprehensible as
goodness? I want to be careful to say that there is no outside
standard of goodness to which God must submit. Nor do
I want to suggest that humans get to decide what is good
and what is not. We are often wrong about what is good
and what is evil. I do want to suggest that since God is holy,
God's self-disclosure must be internally consistent; it must
be honest. God has revealed Godself to be good in Jesus
Christ. God's goodness in Jesus Christ was not revealed as
the God who caused people's suffering. Jesus healed people.
God revealed Godself in Jesus not as the One who gains
glory by causing suffering but as the One who gains glory by

the shame of the cross. Self-consistency means that God can only be what Jesus Christ reveals God to be: good.

Somewhere Between

How are we to carve the path between omnicausality and Deism? We do so by looking at one of the oldest and most important biblical narratives: the fall in Genesis 3. Karl Barth describes the creation narrative as God gaining victory over chaos. I prefer to think of the creation narrative as God putting a barrier between humans and chaos. Settled in the life of the garden, Adam and Eve lived without fear of chaos. Everything was controlled and ordered. When Adam and Eve sinned, they were forced out of the garden and plunged into a world where chaos could strike at any moment. The ground was cursed so that the work humans did for survival would be frustrated, childbirth became painful, and death became reality. The world of the garden—safe, predictable—became the world of chaos—wild, uncertain.

We can also note some important New Testament texts about the governance of earth. The Bible calls the evil one "the Prince and the Power of the Air" and, shockingly, "the god of this world." While the Bible does argue for the providential power of God and notes God's Lordship over earth, one cannot discount the power of evil in the world.

Because of God's goodness, we note that nothing can occur outside God's power. There is no event that God will not work for the good of God's people. The good God seeks, however, is not creature comfort. It is Christlikeness. The good may not be visible during human life. It may only be known in eternity. So saying that God will transform evil into good may often be an act of faith. It still is for me.

For now, it is enough for me to conclude that God is good. God is gracious. God is merciful. God is not the cause of evil. While God may allow God's children to suffer, God never wills them harm. God's goodness is unimpeachable. God's mercy is unfathomable. When it comes to evil, God does not cause it. God corrects it, in this life or the next.

CHAPTER 8

Seeing Things as They Are

One of the great difficulties I had during this time of darkness was correctly viewing my life. It was as if the darkness swallowed up all of the light. I could no longer see all of the goodness God has given me. Learning to see my life as a whole was a step toward healing. When I take a look at my life, I know I am a blessed man.

George Henry Wallace

My ability to love God in the darkness was shaped by remembering something I have always known but had forgotten: I am a lucky man. Scientists who study such things estimate that more than 100 billion humans have lived on planet Earth. In looking at my life, I estimate that I have been among the luckiest of them. My story is full of the goodness of God.

I was born the grandson of George Henry Wallace, "Papa." Papa was born in 1920 in poverty. His mother, Icyanne Lee Wallace, was a Lumbee, which is a Native American tribe that still cannot get federal recognition. The technical term for that now, I believe, is marginalized. Growing up poor necessitated interesting choices in Papa's family. Papa used to love to skip school as any young boy would, but he discovered that he would not get in trouble for it if he brought home dinner. When he was as young as seven, Papa would take his rifle with him to hunt for dinner when he skipped. He used to talk about his "sixth grade education." In fact, he had little formal education at all. No doubt this is why he would ask me every day after school, "What did you learn today?" He would get pretty frustrated if I said, "Nothing."

Papa was a handsome man. The oldest picture I have of him is from his early adulthood. He has his arm around his mother's neck. He is rail thin. He was about 6 feet tall, so I estimate that he was about 140 pounds at the time. I cannot see the flecks of green I remember in his dark eyes, as the picture is black and white. His wavy black hair is slightly mussed, and a big grin is on his face. As I look at the photo, I wonder what was happening when it was taken. Was Papa telling his mother about Nelle, his future wife and my grandmother? Was he celebrating the end of the war? Was he just home on a visit? He was very happy.

The intensity of the Great Depression forged Papa's outlook. As it was for many of his generation, the Great Depression was a scarring event that shaped him for life. Because of the fear he learned in the Depression, he held on to his savings as best he could. He also learned to despise debt. When others were taking on long-term debt to purchase houses, he took a second job to get out of debt quickly. He used to tell me of fistfights over shovels and of cooking wild onions that sprouted up in the yard. He learned to be tough, frugal, tenacious, and industrious.

World War II brought heroism out of him. Papa started the war as a drill sergeant and never would have gone into combat had he not liked to drink, so the family story goes. Apparently, he marched his men into a tree during a training exercise, and with that he was shipped off to the Pacific theater. I only know the story of how Papa earned one of his two Bronze Stars. Papa's unit was on high ground as the Japanese soldiers advanced on their position. The soldier who was supposed to fire the water-cooled machine gun froze in fright. He could not find the resolve to pull the trigger or the wisdom to run. So my grandfather took off his own helmet and hit his fellow soldier with it until he got access to the gun. There he defended his unit from the Japanese onslaught. He faced the rest of his life the way he faced the enemy. He was relentlessly brave.

Papa used to tell me that he was offered a promotion to lieutenant but "did not have the education." That was his way of saying his literacy skills were too limited. Do not think he was unintelligent. He was one of the brightest men I have ever known. He built his own houses with his own hands, built multiple businesses, and crafted a good life for his family. I am a beneficiary of his intelligence and wisdom. If he were alive today, he would be the first person I would call regarding any financial decision or any other decision really. He lacked no intelligence. He lacked educational opportunity.

Despite not having educational opportunities, he made a good way through life. When he got back home from the war, he started a bar with one of his good friends, Ernest Spivey. Spivey, as we called him, was connected to Papa all of his life. Spivey called Papa "Blade" until the day Papa died. I always wanted to know the origin of that nickname, although I was afraid to ask. I'm told it had something to do with running the bar. Apparently there would be fights when the bar ran out of booze for the evening. I'm not sure whether Papa actually pulled a blade, if he only threatened to, if it was just a cool nickname, or if it was the kind of name one assumes to intimidate a would-be assailant. "Don't mess with Blade."

The bar ran its course, and Papa went on to other pursuits. Eventually, he started Wallace and Son's Tire Center. This business provided well for my family for three generations. It was a growing and thriving business. Papa never impressed on me the need to run it in the future, though. He wanted me to have the educational opportunities he never had.

I wish he were here right now to see my life. I am a first-generation university graduate. I have earned a master's degree. I have earned two doctorates. All of my educational opportunities were possible because of his wisdom and entrepreneurial expertise. As I look at the sheepskin on my wall, I wonder what he would have thought of it. Would he know that I think of him every time I look at my diplomas? Would he know how profoundly grateful I am for all he did? Would he know just how proud I am of him?

After his funeral, I went looking through some of his papers and found his discharge papers from the military. It was only then that I discovered he had earned Bronze Stars during combat. I had no idea. When I was little, I used to ask him about the war. Little boys are often curious about such things. I asked if he had won any medals. He told me that he was injured by some shrapnel and could have won the Purple Heart. He turned it down, however. He thought his family would hear of the Purple Heart and think he had died in combat. I never knew of his heroism until after he died. For that omission, I told my dad, "If he were alive, I would have killed him."

After my discovery, our family contacted our US senator to see if we could get Papa's medals. We were delighted by the positive response. Now in my office, below the flag that draped his coffin, is a picture of him and his many medals.

One hundred billion humans have lived on planet Earth, and out of all of these people, George Henry Wallace was my grandfather. I am a blessed man.

Ruth Speight

My maternal grandmother, Ruth Speight, was a courageous person in her own right. Grandmama did not have to face the onslaught of the Japanese; she had to face grinding poverty. She was the mother of four children, and my mother was the youngest. Abandoned by her husband, Grandmama was left to parent four small children alone. Living in the mill village in Rockingham, North Carolina, her prospects were not good. She had to find a way to parent the children and provide for their needs all alone. Work at the mill paid poorly, and hours were not easy to come by. The grind of poverty meant that providing for her children was a daily struggle. I have no memory of her husband, my maternal grandfather. I think this is in part because of the damage his failure to pay child support did to his relationship with my mother. I don't even remember his name being spoken in my house.

When my mother was three years old, my grandmother made the most painful decision any mother could make. She took her four children to an orphanage outside Bedford, Virginia, and left them there. She simply could not earn enough money to make sure they were fed and housed. The older children have memories of the time in the orphanage, mostly unpleasant. I'm not sure my mother remembered much of it. She never spoke about it to me. It was not until after my mother's death that I found out about their time in the orphanage. Even then, it was something to be whispered.

Years later, as my grandmother had become very ill, the remaining family was called to her bedside. There I showed Grandmama a picture of her and her four children that I had found, my mother included. Grandmama told me that picture was taken on the worst day of her life. It was at the orphanage the day she left her children. To her last day, her eyes expressed deep hurt at having to leave her children at the orphanage. The fact that she somehow found the resolve and the resources to bring her children home again is truly an act of courage. While Grandmama and her children struggled, they were together. For them, that was enough.

Of all the people who have ever lived, Ruth Speight was my grandmother. I am a lucky man.

Alice Marie Speight Wallace

My mother, Marie, developed the spunk and attitude of someone who earned every single thing she had. Despite her difficult childhood, Mom ended up going to a community college to study nursing and eventually became a social worker. When she met my father, he was driving a shiny new gold Mercury Cyclone with a 428-cubic-inch engine. It was a serious hot rod. That car could generate greenhouse gas at idle and smoke tires with ease. Dad saw Mom, stopped, and asked if she wanted a ride. This was long before the days when people would be terrified of such an offer. She said "yes." Months later when he pulled out a ring, she said "yes" again.

My parents escaped a life of poverty by hard work and thrift. I will always remember the day they paid off their home. Mom looked at me and said, "We may not have much, but everything we have is ours. No one can take it away." For a woman who was too poor growing up even to have a pet dog, that meant a lot.

For Mom, tenacity was everything. She did dote on me when I was a kid, but she also had real fears for me. I was a quiet little guy with a mischievous streak, but I "let people run over me," as Mom put it. She was always afraid that I would not stand up for myself. As I grew into a teenager, I sometimes got in trouble at school for fighting. When I had to report my troubles to Mom, she would ask, "Did you win?"

Now, I may not have gotten in trouble at home for fighting, but I got in serious trouble for bad grades. Bringing home a bad grade to Mom was brutal. She would not have it. She was determined that I would do well in school, my desires notwithstanding. This was not the determination of today's helicopter moms who rebuke teachers for their children's bad grades. No, if I brought home a bad grade, Mom would "have my hide." I and I alone was responsible. My older sister and I learned a trick to avoiding Mom's wrath when we did not meet her academic expectations. As soon as we got the news, we would find a way to break away and use the school phone to call Dad. He would call Mom and tell her the news. That way, she would have a few hours to blow off steam before she got to us. If we gave her the news when we got home and she had no time to process . . . well, it was most unpleasant.

One of the great tragedies of my life is that my mother passed away young. She was forty-seven. I was not quite twenty-four. Breast cancer robbed my family of her spunk, wisdom, and kindness. I wish she were here. There is so much of my life she missed—my ordination, my graduation from seminary, the births of my children. I would have loved to reach out to her on that terrible day when I collapsed. I think of her daily even now. She was simply amazing.

Billions of women have had the privilege of being a mother. I was born to a wonderful, spunky, tenacious woman named Marie. I am a lucky man.

Jim Wallace

My father Jim is the only one of this cast still living. Dad is a big man physically and metaphorically. Standing 6-foot-2 and over 260 pounds of thick muscle, Dad is an imposing character. He is so imposing that people in our hometown often call him "Big Jim." Dad is a man of great faith. His lifelong ambition is to serve the church, and he is most dissatisfied if he is not teaching a Sunday school class or serving as a deacon. It was from Dad that I first learned the subtleties of Christian doctrine. It was from him that I learned how to love God with my mind. His contributions to my faith are legion.

Dad and Mom created a solid middle-class home for me and my three sisters. We all had every educational opportunity we wanted. All of us attended college. Among the four of us there are three bachelor's degrees, two master's degrees, and two doctorates. Had Jenni's life not been cut short, there would have been more degrees, I'm sure. In short, we all had the opportunity to create the life we desired. We had opportunities that our parents rarely even dreamed of for themselves.

When Mom died, Dad was left to parent two thirteen-year-old daughters, no easy feat even in the best of circumstances. Every day before work, he stood in the hallway between the two doors of the girls' rooms and prayed a blessing over them. He stood before God, asking for God's care, protection, and blessing. I'm sure he also had to pray for patience as teenage girls can be *tough*! He managed to parent them both with love and grace, even alone.

Dad has taught me many lessons. He taught me to be mentally strong, to be unyielding in the face of pressure, to withstand and outlast every obstacle. He taught me never to make decisions when I am angry or in a heightened emotional state. One of the best lessons he taught me, however, was courage. I can only hope I have as much courage as he does.

Jim Wallace is a heroic figure, and I am fortunate that he is my dad.

The Luckiest Man Alive

On July 4, 1939, Lou Gehrig gave one of the most famous speeches in sports history. In talking about the disease he had been diagnosed with, the one that would eventually bear his name, the Yankee great said,

> Fans, for the past two weeks you have been reading about the bad break I got. Yet today I consider myself the luckiest man on the face of this earth. I have been in ballparks for seventeen years and have never received anything but kindness and encouragement from you fans.
>
> Look at these grand men. Which of you wouldn't consider it the highlight of his career just to associate with them for even one day? Sure, I'm lucky. Who wouldn't consider it an honor to have known Jacob Ruppert? Also, the builder of baseball's greatest empire, Ed Barrow? To have spent six years with that wonderful little fellow, Miller Huggins? Then to have spent the next nine years with that outstanding leader, that smart student of psychology, the best manager in baseball today, Joe McCarthy? Sure, I'm lucky.

When the New York Giants, a team you would give your right arm to beat and vice versa, sends you a gift—that's something. When everybody down to the groundskeepers and those boys in white coats remember you with trophies—that's something. When you have a wonderful mother-in-law who takes sides with you in squabbles with her own daughter—that's something. When you have a father and a mother who work all their lives so you can have an education and build your body—it's a blessing. When you have a wife who has been a tower of strength and shown more courage than you dreamed existed—that's the finest I know.

So, I close in saying that I may have had a tough break, but I have an awful lot to live for.[37]

When I look at what my grandparents suffered and accomplished, and when I look at what my parents gave me, I know just how radically blessed I am. Among the billions of people who have ever lived on planet Earth, few of them have had it better than me. In truth, all of my needs have been met and most of my wants have been met. So most of my days should be spent in humble gratitude. I know in my heart that most people who have ever lived would gladly trade their lives for mine, tragic losses included. When I am honest with myself, I have to concur with Gehrig: I am the luckiest man alive. It was difficult to remember my great good fortune when I was sinking in the darkness. Keeping it in mind, however, would have helped me hold on to some glimmer of light.

Epilogue

As much as I wanted time to stand still in the aftermath of Jenni's loss, time never does. It moves inexorably forward despite our desires. When everything in us is screaming for the world to freeze and notice the absence created in our lives, to honor our emptiness, the world does not. It keeps spinning on its axis and rotating in its elliptical orbit around the sun. While we do not recognize it at the time, this is for our good. Remaining stuck at the point of our loss means we remain stuck in our grief. I do not, however, believe time heals all wounds. No, all healing comes from God, but most often healing takes time.

In reality, I'm not sure I have healed much since Jenni died, now fourteen years ago. I do not know how to measure healing anymore. Is healing measured in absence of tears, in the end of the dark cloud covering all life? Is it measured in the ability to laugh again or hope again or trust again? I am not sure. I do know that my life is different and better than it was on the day I collapsed. I do know that the man who fell to the floor in a pile of flesh is not the man I am now. And that is good.

Josh will always have a special place in my heart. I made sure to tell him that the last time we spoke. I cannot speak with him often. Once we end our talks, I am a wreck. It is like knowing that the biggest thing we have in common is gone. Eventually, our shared loss must come up in our conversation. Every time it does, though, the wound reopens. It is enough for me to see his life at a distance and know that it is good. Josh has remarried. His wife is an art teacher, and they have a precious little girl with the curliest brown hair I have ever seen. For all the sorrow that he experienced, I pray that he will have double the joys. It looks as if he is on the way.

Judi struggled the most after Jenni's death. She had never lived a day without her twin sister before. Now, not only would she live every remaining day without her but every birthday would be a cause for mourning and remembering, and every holiday would be evidence of what had gone wrong. In short, it was brutal. Judi, however, demonstrated amazing courage. She found her footing. She graduated nursing school. Eventually, she earned a master's in nursing. I, of course, am very proud of her accomplishments. She married in 2014 and is now the mother of twins, a boy and a girl.

Dad finally remarried, and I had the privilege of officiating his wedding. In perfect keeping with his character, Elvis's music was played for his wedding processional. I enjoy remembering that. He now has a whole cadre of grandkids. He loves being a grandad, and his grandchildren adore him. Some of the grandkids call him "Papa," others "Big Pop." He is a giant figure in their lives, as it should be.

In 2014 I met the amazing Molly Rushing. Although we had never met previously, our lives had been intertwined for years. My predecessor at the church I served before coming to Rosemary served as her interim pastor. The contemporary worship leader at the church where Molly served as minister of youth had previously served as my minister of music. Oddly enough, the then music minister at Rosemary had a daughter who served as Molly's predecessor. If all that were not enough, Molly's father and I were friends in seminary. Even odder, Molly's brother served as the music minister at the church I briefly attended while I was in seminary. How Molly and I did not know each other before 2014 still strikes us both as odd. Life, however, can be odd. So, on an April evening, Molly and I met for the first time at a Chili's restaurant. We talked for hours. I'm sure our server wanted us to vacate her table, but we were fairly oblivious. The conversation was too good to vacate. In October of that year, I proposed. Against all the best wisdom in the Western Hemisphere, she said "yes." In June 2015, we married. We now have two precious, precocious little girls together who light up our lives and our faces. They say that being around small children will keep you young. They lie. It mostly keeps you sleepy, but it is a good sleepy.

The darkness has broken. Light has reemerged. There are days when I can still feel the cold darkness creeping in, but God has given me so much grace that the darkness can be dispelled. It is my hope that the goodness of God will dispel your darkness too. Until then, I hope you can love God even in the darkness.

Notes

1. HIPAA is the Health Insurance Portability and Accountability Act. It created federal standards for the sharing of personal health information.

2. I do not want to suggest that all of the doctors were terrible. They were not. They were all excellent physicians. Their bedside manner and their arrogant demeanor, however, were on full display during Jenni's hospitalization. There was one exception—Dr. Katz. He was not only excellent but also compassionate. He was good to the family, particularly Judi. He knew Judi was taking time off from her nursing program to be with Jenni and had witnessed her potential as a nurse. So he offered to write letters of recommendation for Judi to help her get back into the nursing program.

3. I also do not want to have anyone think that I believe all nurses behave like the one I am describing. Almost all nurses are exceptional people. They do difficult work, often under extreme duress. The excellent nature of most nurses makes this particular nurse's behavior stick out more. For some reason, he wanted to fight with me. He escalated the argument at every opportunity and refused to let me just walk away.

4. Since I do not create manuscripts of my sermons, this is a reconstruction of what I said on that day.

5. Thomas Long, "Words, Words, Words," *Princeton Seminary Bulletin* (1991): 318.

6. Kate Bowler, *Everything Happens for a Reason and Other Lies I've Loved* (New York: Random House, 2018), 121–22.

7. C. S. Lewis, *A Grief Observed* (New York: Bantam Books, 1961), 4.

8. Vicky Reddish, "How Did the Great Smoky Mountains Get Their Name?" *SmokyMountains.com*, November 15, 2009, smokymountains. com/park/blog/great-smoky-mountains-get-name/.

9. Ibid.

10. Matthew Hoffman, MD, "Picture of the Brain," *WebMD*, reviewed June 3, 2021, webmd.com/brain/picture-of-the-brain#1.

11. Elizabeth Armstrong Moore, "Human Brain Has More Switches than All Computers on Earth," *CNET*, November 17, 2010, cnet.com/ news/human-brain-has-more-switches-than-all-computers-on-earth/.

12. Chris Baraniuk, "The Enormous Power of the Unconscious Brain," *BBC*, March 16, 2016, bbc.com/future/article/20160315 -the-enormous-power-of-the-unconscious-brain.

13. Ibid.

14. Moore, "Human Brain Has More Switches."

15. "The Human Brain Is the Most Complex Structure," *Independent*, April 2, 2014, independent.co.uk/voices/editorials/ human-brain-most-complex-structure-universe-let-s-do-all-we-can- unravel-its-mysteries-9233125.html.

16. Helen Phillips, "Introduction: The Human Brain," NewScientist, September 4, 2006, newscientist.com/article/dn9969-introduction-the- human-brain/.

17. "December 26, 2004: Tsunami Devastates Indian Ocean Coast," *History*, November 13, 2009, history.com/this-day-in-history/ tsunami-devastates-indian-ocean-coast.

18. David Roos, "The 2004 Tsunami Wiped Away Towns with 'Mind-boggling' Destruction," *History*, October 2, 2018, history.com/ news/deadliest-tsunami-2004-indian-ocean.

19. David Roos, "The 2004 Tsunami Wiped Away Towns with 'Mind-boggling' Destruction," *History*, October 2, 2018, history.com/ news/deadliest-tsunami-2004-indian-ocean.

20. David Bentley Hart, *The Doors of the Sea: Where Was God in the Tsunami?* (Grand Rapids: Eerdmans, 2005), 99.

21. "The Great Lisbon Earthquake and Tsunami, Portugal" SMS Tsunami Warning, sms-tsunami-warning.com/pages/tsunami- portugal-1755, accessed February 15, 2016.

22. William J. Broad, "Deadly and Yet Necessary, Quakes Renew the Planet," *New York Times*, January 11, 2005, nytimes.com/2005/01/11/science/deadly-and-yet-necessary-quakes-renew-the-planet.html.

23. Jean Calvin and Henry Beveridge, *Institutes of the Christian Religion* (Grand Rapids: Eerdmans, 1989), book 3, ch. 23, sec. 8, 232.

24. Theologians refer to evil that occurs not because of a choice "natural evil." Natural evil includes disease, natural disasters, and naturally occurring death.

25. "Friendships: Enrich Your Life and Improve Your Health," *Mayo Clinic*, January 12, 2022, mayoclinic.org/healthy-lifestyle/adult-health/in-depth/friendships/art-20044860.

26. Ibid.

27. Walter Brueggemann, Spirituality of the Psalms (Minneapolis: Fortress, 2002), 8.

28. Brueggemann, *Spirituality of the Psalms*, viii.

29. Brueggemann, *Spirituality of the Psalms*, 8.

30. C. S. Lewis, *Reflections on the Psalms* (New York: Harper Collins, 1958), 73.

31. David Bentley Hart, *The Experience of God: Being, Consciousness, Bliss* (New Haven: Yale University Press, 2013), 253–54.

32. Hart, *The Experience of God*, 253–54.

33. Karl Barth, *Word of God and the Word of Man*, trans. Douglas Horton (London: Hodder and Stoughton, 1928), 196; Jean Calvin and Henry Beveridge, *Institutes of the Christian Religion* (Grand Rapids Eerdmans, 1989), 97.

34. Hart, *Doors of the Sea*, 54.

35. Bowler, *Everything Happens for a Reason*, 114.

36. Alister E. McGrath, ed., *The Christian Theology Reader* (Oxford: Blackwell, 1999), 12.

37. "Full Text of Lou Gehrig's Farewell Speech," *Sports Illustrated*, July 4, 2009, si.com/mlb/2009/07/05/gehrig-text.

www.ingramcontent.com/pod-product-compliance
Lightning Source LLC
Chambersburg PA
CBHW072355090426
42741CB00012B/3040